Barbara Johannah's Crystal Piecing

“For many years I have considered Barbara Johannah the forerunner of quick-piecing in America. As progressive quilters in the 20th century, we owe her many thanks and much gratitude.”

Georgia J. Bonesteel, TV hostess
Lap Quilting With Georgia Bonesteel
Hendersonville, NC

“Barbara's innovative techniques go from her books to teachers to students...a case where the "trickle-down" theory actually works and benefits everybody.”

Jean Ray Laury, author
Imagery on Fabric
Clovis, CA

“All quilters who do quick piecing owe a great debt to Barbara Johannah. She, more than anyone else I can think of, is responsible for starting our wheels turning to the possibilities of strip piecing. Her original ideas were the beginnings of the many spin-offs that have taken the quilting world by storm.”

Kaye Wood, TV hostess
Quilting for the '90's
West Branch, MI

“I'm delighted to learn that Barbara Johannah's books will once again be available to the quilting world. Barbara was a true pioneer in quick quiltmaking techniques that have influenced thousands of busy quiltmakers to enter the field.”

Karey P. Bresenhan, President
Quilt Market
Houston, TX

“Barbara's contribution to quiltmaking was early and far-reaching. I remember exactly how I felt when I read her quick-quilting solution to Half-Square Triangles—I thought this was the most innovative thing I had ever heard of and wished I had thought of it myself. I adopted it promptly.”

Virginia Avery, author
Wonderful Wearables
Port Chester, NY

Warning!
This book is content-rich! Consume in small doses over a long period of time!

" Grandma Meda never wrote a book nor made a quilt, but I think much of what I can do came through her. A story my mother tells illustrates why I feel this way.

My mother was visiting cousins for a month. While there, she saw a picture in a newspaper of a dress she liked. Wanting such a dress, she tore out the picture, bought some fabric, and sent both to her mother.

Mom's cousins were incredulous. They felt Mom was being unrealistic to expect her mother to make a dress for her without a pattern and without her being available for fittings.

Mom didn't see any problem. Mom expected Grandma Meda to make the dress the way she always did— cut the fabric out freehand, without a pattern, without measuring, without even a fitting.

No matter how complex the design, Grandma Meda always cut the pieces out freehand. She had no use for patterns and her garments always fit beautifully. That dress, finished and fitting perfectly, was sent to my mom at her cousin's, much to their amazement.

Not until years later did my mom realize the magnitude of Grandma Meda's ability. I appreciate it also. I cannot imagine being able to cut out by eye.

Outside the family, no one knows what Grandma could do. **"**

Acknowledgments

I wish to thank the whole crew who works with Robbie: Rosalie Cooke, Martha Vercoutere, Gil and Kaarli Bowers, Pam Poole, and Rosalyn Carson. And Robbie Fanning, the only editor I know who would have a vision of what the book should be. I submitted a manuscript and truly, Robbie and her crew created a book.

I would like to thank Pat Whittemore's quilt group for playing with Crystal Piecing, especially Marlene Andrey, Marge Couch, and Pat Whittemore, as well as Beckie Olson, Linda Fry Kenzle, and Pat Cairns. Thank you to Sharon Hose and Pat Whittemore for making quilts. Thanks, too, to all the artists and writers who took time to send a note about my earlier work.

I wish to thank my parents as always, Mother for correcting the English language portion and Father for going over the math portion and challenging me on everything. I also wish to thank my husband and son for accepting the duration. For help with new computer programs, I wish to thank Paul Turnbull, Pam Manley, Loren Amalang, and especially Sharon Gowan.

Barbara Johannah's Crystal Piecing

Hidden Treasures
Border designed by Jane Warnick

Barbara Johannah

Chilton Book Company
Radnor, Pennsylvania

Publication History of Barbara Johannah

1976: *Quick Quilting—Make a Quilt This Weekend* (Out of Print). This first book on quick machine methods contains directions for piecing traditional pattterns.

1979: Self-published *Quick Quiltmaking Handbook*. Covers the new methods for fast and simple piecing that cuts the time to make a pieced quilt top from months to days.

1980: Self-published *Continuous Curve Quilting—Machine Quilting the Pieced Quilt*. A method of machine quilting pieced patterns that is adapted to the unique abilities of sewing machines.

1987: Self-published *Half Square Triangles—Exploring Design*. This book weaves together the creative discoveries of a 17th Century monk and 20th Century quilts. The design system is infinite.

Copyright © 1993 by Barbara Johannah

All Rights Reserved

Published in Radnor, Pennsylvania 19089, by Chilton Book Company

Designer: Martha Vercoutere

Illustrators: Pamela S. Poole, Barbara Johannah

Editors: Robbie Fanning, Rosalie Cooke, Gil Bowers

Quilters: Pat Whittemore, Sharon Hose

Photographer: Lee Lindeman

Cover quilt designed by Rosalyn Carson, pieced, and machine-quilted by Pat Whittemore

Manufactured in the United States of America
Printed on acid-free paper

Library of Congress Catalog Card Number 92-54914

ISBN 0-8019-8400-9

1 2 3 4 5 6 7 8 9 0   2 1 0 9 8 7 6 5 4 3

Foreword by Robbie Fanning

The word "paradigm" means a model accepted by a community to explain a concept.

For hundreds of years we all believed the earth was flat. Mothers warned children not to venture far or "you'll fall off the edge of the earth."

Then it was discovered and proved that the earth was round. Wonderment! Awe! We began to think in new ways and the round model became our paradigm. We had experienced a paradigm shift.

Not all paradigm shifts are so grand but they still change our day-to-day activities. For example, the paradigm shift that led to workable sewing machines happened in 1755 when Charles Weisenthal made a needle pointed at both ends. No particular notice was paid to this discovery, but seventy-five years later, it led Walter Hunt to realize the eye of the needle must be located in the pointed end, not the thick end, as in hand sewing—and we had our first real sewing machine.

It seems obvious now—*of course* the eye must be in the pointed end!—but that's the nature of a paradigm shift. Those who have the old model imprinted in their brains are sluggish to change their thinking. It's hard to make the switch to a new image, a new procedure. Those who are introduced to the new paradigm can't imagine why people stick to the old ways.

The ideas of the people who force the paradigm shift are usually not quickly accepted. Then someone will come along who sees the potential and knows how to exploit it—and we all rush to follow that new path. My image of the process is of a flowing river. Someone digs a small canal through the bank and water begins to flow away from the main channel. After a time, the entry enlarges and suddenly, the river changes course and follows the canal. The canal becomes the river. Most of us are like logs in the river, floating along the main channel until the current carries us another way.

The quilting world experienced a paradigm shift in the middle 1970s, with the publication of Barbara Johannah's first books. (Incidentally, it's pronounced *Yo-HAWN-ah.*) Until then, we cut little shapes of fabric, resewed them into blocks, and sewed the blocks together to make a quilt. Barbara, inspired by Seminole piecing, realized "Whole cloth! We must work with whole cloth, not little pieces!" She then developed fast, easy ways to make most traditional quilt patterns.

It's hard to believe that her methods were not accepted at first. Today, methods like strip piecing have become our paradigm.

People who force paradigm shifts are originals; Barbara hasn't stopped thinking and experimenting. This book brings together and updates her three most important contributions to quilting: working with whole cloth, Continuous Curve Quilting, and an approach to designing quilts. I believe we're going to see another paradigm shift in quilting when people grasp the implications of her recent explorations, particularly of Jewels in Crystal Piecing (see page 58) and of equilateral triangles (see page 127).

This book is dense, informative, inspiring, and thought-provoking. Working on it has been a privilege.

Barbara and I would like to see what you come up with after reading this book. Please send snapshots to Barbara Johannah, c/o Open Chain Publishing, Inc., PO Box 2634, Menlo Park, CA 94026.

Prepare to change course.

Contents

How I Discovered Quick Quiltmaking

When I began making my first quilt in the mid-1960's, I hadn't actually ever seen one before. The whole of my knowledge consisted of having seen an occasional glimpse of a quilt on the cowboy movies I had watched on television as a child. While in junior college, I took an interior-decorating class. We were required to sew something for the home. Not wanting to make curtains and such, I decided to make a quilt. First I checked the library, but there weren't any books on quilts. I asked my mother if she knew how. As a child, she had watched older women make quilts, but she hadn't learned herself. It wasn't valued when she grew up.

Undaunted by my lack of knowledge, I plunged in. I wished to make a quilt of fancy fabrics, satins, velvets, and moirés. I collected sewing scraps, bought remnants, and purchased dresses from the Salvation Army to get enough fabric. I didn't have the slightest idea how to proceed, but began to cut up fabric into odd-shaped pieces. I turned under the edges of each piece and pinned them. Then I basted them under. Then I basted them to a sheet, overlapping the patches. Finally I used embroidery floss to feather stitch around each piece of fabric.

What with all the turning under and layering of fabric, in some places I needed pliers to pull the needle through. I worked diligently all of the six weeks allotted to the project, including Christmas vacation. Progress was so slow you couldn't see it day to day. Mother would come home from work and say, "I thought you were going to work on the quilt today" after I had just spent several hours working on the quilt. I feared the teacher would fail me. Fortunately she knew more about how long it takes to make a quilt than I did. After the semester was over, I put away

the unfinished quilt. I now knew how I *should* have made it. (That was the beginning of a succession of never-finished quilts, because once I figured out how I should have made them, I quit. I did finish the first quilt—five years later.)

I located a copy of Ruby McKim's *101 Quilt Patterns,* Ruth Finley's *Old Patchwork Quilts and the Women Who Made Them,* and Margaret Ickis' *The Standard Book of Quilt Making and Collecting,* all that was available at that time. I pored over them, absorbing every quilt pattern. Gradually, I developed a good working knowledge of traditional piecing and refined my ideas of how to work efficiently using the sewing machine. I also started teaching at the YWCA.

A big breakthrough came when I read an article on the Seminole Indians of Florida. It described how the US Government had given the people long inch-wide strips of cloth. Necessity being the mother of invention, the Seminole people ingeniously had sewn the strips together, cut crosswise, and resewn these pieces to make complex, multicolored, decorative fabric for clothing. The article had a drawing of the process.

I looked at that drawing and—eureka!—it plugged in with the hundreds of quilt patterns in my head. Pattern after traditional pattern combined with the idea of using strips instead of individual templates to make them. It was like fireworks in my head. For about five minutes I was oblivious of my surroundings and aware only of the mental explosions going on in my head.

It was a Peak Experience, as Maslow calls it. When it was over, I knew—I simply knew.

What was left was to figure out the math. Seminole patchwork is sewn without mathematical precision. Pieces are intentionally offset. Corners intentionally don't meet. The challenge was how to take the idea of Seminole and adapt it to the precision of quiltmaking. I began to use the basic Seminole idea to develop a mathematically precise way of doing quilt patterns.

Along the way, I learned of Ernest B. Haight of David City, NE. Educated as an engineer, he was unable to find work in this field during the Depression, so he returned to the family farm. Over the years, first helping his wife and then on his own, he designed and pieced quilts. He understood that machine piecing should be done using whole cloth as a grid system rather than using the template system to cut individual small pieces. In the mid-1970's he published a brief booklet suggesting the possibilities of machine piecing. He didn't work with strips at all. He used whole cloth. As far as I know, he was the first to do Half-Square Triangles with this method. He also devised a unique method of machine quilting rectangular quilts (see page 150). Because he was not active in the quilt revival, Mr. Haight's accomplishments did not receive wide exposure.

As I worked out the math for quilt pattern after quilt pattern, I extended the idea of working with whole cloth rather than templates to new methods— Quarter-Square Triangles, Snowball, and more. I taught more classes at the YWCA and in adult school as well. I taught both traditional template piecing and the new methods I was devising.

One day in a fabric store, I fell into conversation with a clerk. She told me about the quilt she was making. Wanting to help, I started to tell her how to make it faster. She stopped me. She said, "If you really have a new method that hasn't been written up in any quilt books, I don't want to know about it. You go home and write a book about it."

So I did. Thinking up the methods had been easy. Writing the book proved to be extremely difficult. Not knowing how to begin I asked the librarian at our local public library. He suggested going through the quilt books on the shelves. (This was now the early 1970's. The quilt revival had begun, so there were some quilt books on the shelves.) While I enjoyed every one of the existing books and got a lot out of them, they wouldn't do as models for my book. They all talked about quilts, but they didn't actually tell you how to make one. I was on my own.

My inspiration came from an unexpected source. My husband was working on our car. Not being familiar with Volkswagen buses, an early type of van, he had purchased the book *How to Keep Your Volkswagen Alive and Well, A Step by Step Manual for the Complete Idiot*. I was impressed. There he was out in the garage making major repairs to a car by following the instructions in a book. This had to be a well-written book, the kind of book I wanted to write.

I then realized that I wanted the cookbook model: step one, step two, in explaining a process. My book would need to be explained in diagrams, as well as in words. The text had to be clear enough to stand alone. The drawings had to be extensive enough to explain

" I have been quilting since 1974 and recall all too clearly the sparse information and tools available to quilters at that time. The only books that were in print were oriented to a 19th century approach. For those of us with sewing-machine skills, the implied suggestion was to abandon technology and pick up a hand-held needle and thread.

The only voice in this vacuum of sewing savvy was Barbara Johannah. Her simple, concise approach brought quiltmaking into the 20th century. *Quick Quiltmaking Handbook* led the way to all the template-free approaches to patchwork, *Half Square Triangles/Exploring Design* solves the problems of working with stripes and prints, and *Continuous Curve Quilting* is the clear foundation of all machine-quilting instructions that followed. Barbara showed us all how and put us on the right road. **"**

Linda Denner, author
Baby Quilts
Garden City, NY

> " I would like Barbara to receive credit for her ingenious contribution to quiltmaking. Barbara's fast piecing and cutting methods have revolutionized quiltmaking and made modern-day work much faster and more accurate. I'm glad her work is being documented, not letting it get so absorbed that we forget who gave us the technique that now appears everywhere. "
>
> Diane Leone, owner
> The Quilting Bee
> Mountain View, CA

> " Patents protect inventions, copyrights protect words, but lady, there ain't nothing sacred about an idea. "

the method. Together, text and drawings must convey these new methods. I was fortunate in that I had been teaching, so I knew for whom I was writing. I knew what the quilt book buyer would be likely to know and not know. My mother's an excellent editor and she also helped.

When I had about 40 pages, I bought some paper and printed up copies, but then I thought "Why not approach a trade publisher?" Back to the library. The librarian showed me a volume on publishers, hundreds of them. He advised approaching those who were already in the needlework/craft field, those of some size. I made a list of 50 publishers.

Not knowing how to proceed, I called a literary agent. I wanted to know two things—what was the proper way to approach 50 publishers in a timely way and how could I protect my ideas? I didn't want to send my manuscript to a publisher and have them say "Great new idea! Let's have one of our experienced writers do the book." This was a valid concern as needlework and craft books at that time were written by writers, rather than by people accomplished in the particular field. This was evident from the back covers. They would say "Other Books By Author" and list books on crochet, ceramics, doll houses, découpage, knitting, and baskets. How could one person be an expert in all those fields? I refer to such books as term-paper books: same old material, rewritten, with new photos added. My conversation with the agent was short but important. He said, "Patents protect inventions, copyrights protect words, but lady, there ain't nothing sacred about an idea."

In my personal hierarchy, ideas are most important, but that was beside the point. He had told me briefly, clearly, and to the point the legal standing of a new idea.

His next words were cause for hope. He said rather than send my manuscript out to one publisher at a time and wait two to six months for each to look it over and return it, I could send out a cover letter and one page from the manuscript to all of them at once.

After several weeks the rejections started to come in—form-letter rejections. Even the signatures were mechanically produced. Occasionally I got a hand-signed rejection. On a good day, I got a personally written rejection.

Then one day I got a letter saying, "We want to do your book. We're sending you a contract." After seeing only one page of my manuscript! I was ecstatic.

I added more material to my initial 40 pages and got it up to book length, helped by my mother as editor. But I was a total novice. They said, "Send what you have and we'll help you work on it." They didn't. They published my freehand-drawn geometric drawings as is. I was mortified, embarrassed.

Yet in spite of its poor looks, *Quick Quilting—Make a Quilt This Weekend* sold. And sold and sold. It was their best-selling book of 1976, our Bicentennial year.

What I didn't know was that the publisher was having financial problems. They would sell out a printing of my book and take back orders for months before they could afford to reprint *Quick Quilting* again. They repeated this over and over. Ordinarily this "temporarily out of stock" situation would kill a book, but *Quick Quilting* sold on and on.

They weren't paying me either. When the publisher went into Chapter 11 bankruptcy, they were protected legally from paying me. Since they weren't going to pay me anyway, I signed away what they owed me to get out of the contract and buy back my own book. I felt burned and burned badly. I didn't want anything to do with trade publishers. I figured I couldn't do any worse if I self-published, so I worked on refining and adding new material. Three years later, in 1979, I self-published *Quick Quiltmaking Handbook*.

During that time, I continued to teach locally through the adult school. I also gave workshops and talks at quilt shows and quilt shops across the country. And I had fun. I enjoyed sharing my ideas with others.

I thought people would instantly and enthusiastically grasp the significance of my new methods. But acceptance was slow. More than one national quilting authority looked down her nose at my methods.

I understood, though. Forget the new methods of Strips and Strata and Crystal Piecing. At that time it was revolutionary to machine piece rather than hand piece individual template-cut pieces. The quilt revival was still new—few books, fewer teachers. People can only take in one new idea at a time.

But machine methods gradually caught on. The fact that you couldn't tell if a pieced quilt top had been made by traditional hand-pieced methods or by machine methods had gradually won people over, so that by the time my 1979 book came out there was wide acceptance of machine methods.

"The idea of first marking fabric; then sewing seams; and finally cutting pieces has served me well since I first purchased *Quick Quilting* in 1976. The concepts it contained helped me and many of my students to be faster at piecing while maintaining accuracy. Barbara demonstrated that there is more than one way to accomplish one's work. Flexibility leads to creativity, which produces ultimate joy and pride in accomplishment.

Barbara Johannah has quietly been in the forefront of latter 20th century quiltmaking activity. Her influences have been far-reaching."

Carla Rodio, artist
Hendersonville, NC

Books by Harriet Hargrave:
Heirloom Machine Quilting
Mastering Machine Appliqué
Both published by C&T Publishing.

"It's about time this woman received some of the recognition she deserves. I have been screaming about her work and techniques for years. It didn't start out that way, though. I looked at her first book but felt I would never feel comfortable doing the quick-cutting techniques. I really do everything the long way. But finally I decided to try her techniques. I was very skeptical.

About 8:30 a.m. I read the relevant parts, drew up charts for cutting, and made some cardboard rulers of different widths (this was before rotary cutters and rulers). With great misgivings, I started. I had the whole quilt cut out and the first block made by 11:30 a.m. I couldn't believe it and everything was accurate. I made a complete 80" x 90" quilt in two days. Unbelievable! I have been praising Barbara and her techniques ever since."

Janet B. Elwin, author
Creative Triangles
Damariscotta, ME

Then I had a new experience. One of my students expressed dissatisfaction with the idea of spending hundreds of hours hand quilting a quilt top that had been made in tens of hours. She told me my quick-piecing methods were good, but they were a job half-done. When would I devise a versatile and attractive method of machine quilting, too?

I thought about it, experimented, and came up with Continuous Curve Quilting. The secret was to choose appropriate designs with a strong figure/background relationship, then quilt the background in gentle arcs, going through the corners of adjoining background blocks to minimize starts and stops. (See Chapter 11, page 6, for more information.) My student was impressed. Now the quilt process was complete.

I wrote up my idea, with many examples, in a new book, *Continuous Curve Quilting*, which I self-published in 1981.

Again, I thought people would jump at this new method. Unlike machine piecing, which actually caught on quickly, acceptance of machine quilting was slow. Still, *Continuous Curve Quilting* sold steadily, gradually increasing in sales over the years as more people tried it. The acceptance of machine quilting got a big boost from Harriet Hargrave. She had been experimenting with machine quilting, but was frustrated with the results. Continuous Curve Quilting provided her with the basic framework of how machine quilting should be done. But she added an important element: free-machine quilting. Because I worked with the presser foot on, I didn't machine quilt entire quilts with my method. I quilted blocks or rows. Otherwise, it was too cumbersome to turn the quilt. Harriet used my method with free-machine quilting, enabling all of us to machine quilt entire quilts with Continuous Curve Quilting. She mixed this technique with her extensive experience with machine settings and feet and became a vocal proponent. Much of Continuous Curve Quilting acceptance is due to Harriet Hargrave, who has crisscrossed the country promoting it (along with her beautiful free-machine quilting).

My next adventure came when my friend, Jane Warnick, told me of her exploration of design with half-square triangles, especially applied to quilts. She had come across references to a 17th century monk who was also intrigued with their design possibilities. I suggested she write a book. She suggested *I* write the book. We then started writing together, but because of her husband's declining health, Jane dropped out. I continued and self-published *Half Square Triangles/Exploring Design* in 1987.

With both my piecing book, *Quick Quilting—Make A Quilt This Weekend*, and my machine-quilting book, *Continuous Curve Quilting*, there were no existing markets. The ideas were so innovative that the market developed for the books *after* they were published.

I thought, however, that with the publication of *Half Square Triangles*, I had at last written a commercial book, that it would begin to sell immediately. In this book I went all out—glossy stock and 16 pages of color. It cost a fortune to self-publish.

No such luck. It sold, but at a slow and steady rate, not the big rush I had expected. When I began to get enthusiastic letters from engineers, computer programmers, and high school math teachers instead of from quilters, I realized that once again I had written a book that would take a while to achieve acceptance.

I developed serious health problems and was forced to become fairly inactive in the quilt field. I moved to a rural area that was less poisonous to my body. This gave me the time to reflect and to explore more ideas.

Then Robbie Fanning came to me, wanting to combine and update all of my methods in one book that would receive a much wider distribution than I could achieve in self-publishing. She also knew that my stamina was too low to continue publishing my new methods by myself. She wants the whole world to be exposed to my thoughts and experiments. She can't wait to see what people will do with the newest ideas, like Equilateral Triangles (page 127) and the Snowball concept (page 59).

When I was asked to write this book, five years after my last book, I needed to think about all this again. The where and how of my discoveries was old information. But a new question came to mind. Why was I the person who took the basic idea of the Seminole Indians and fused it with the mathematical precision of quilt piecing? Why was I the individual to develop Continuous Curve Quilting, a method of quilting without precedent?

I've always assumed the answer is "I'm just naturally good at math." I have been blessed with more natural ability in math and spatial reasoning than most. Perhaps only one person in a hundred has more ability than I do. But using a little of that inborn

"Back when people were painstakingly marking and cutting one little fabric piece at a time, Barbara showed us how to simplify, to speed up the boring parts, and to machine stitch quilts in record time. Best of all, she gave us permission to have fun and not take our work too seriously.

When I was first introduced to her *Quick Quiltmaking Handbook*, my creative life changed immediately. I was an overworked, middle-aged wife and mother with a new baby and very little time and energy. Barbara made quilting possible for people like me. She is truly the "mother" of modern quick quiltmaking!"

Jennifer Amor, author
Flavor Quilts for Kids to Make
Columbia, SC

ability, I figured out how many people in the USA alone have more innate ability than I do: at least 2-3 million people. With that many people having more natural ability in these areas than I do, I say, "Why me?"

The second possibility was education. Did an advanced math education explain it? No again. Others are often surprised to hear my math education ended with high school geometry.

If neither natural ability nor formal schooling explain why I've discovered so many timesaving methods for quilters, what does? This question is of particular interest to me because our son is being educated at home.

When I was a child, my father always said, "Think for yourself" or "Do your own thinking," whether it concerned social relationships or school subjects. I remember asking him about the material for an upcoming test. I disagreed with the teachers. Father said, "Put down the answers you believe to be correct, even if you know the teacher will mark your answers wrong." As a result, I never absorbed the concept "To get along, go along." Instead, I learned "Do what you think is right and let the chips fall where they may." I also remember a frustrated teacher telling me "Why won't you put down the 'right answer'? I know that you know it." But I wouldn't put down an answer I thought was wrong merely to please the teacher.

Consequently I was and still am extremely slow. I often take incredible amounts of time to do the simplest things.

So now I think I was the one to devise so many fast piecing and quilting methods because my father taught me to think for myself, to question all knowledge before I make it my own. Quick Quiltmaking is, after all, very simple.

I think of these things while home-schooling my son. I take care that I don't approach education as pouring information into his head, but rather as nurturing the growing ability to think for himself.

Thanks, Dad.

Barbara Johannah
Northern California

How to Use This Book

Minus the prints, the interplay of color, the very fabrics from which quilts are made, the underlying structure of traditional American quilt patterns is also beautiful.

I want to show you how to see the underlying bones, to free you from set instructions for specific quilts, and then to combine that knowledge with the potential of my methods. I want to increase the realm of what is probable, not lock quilters into cookie-cutter quilts.

And yet we are all more comfortable learning one step at a time, starting from what we already know. That's why I've given instructions in this book for specific quilts. People who are unfamiliar with a technique can make a learning sample or quilt. As you gain an understanding of the method, I hope you will think about its potential. Try not to think in narrow categories.

The types of quilts we make are often shaped by the method of making them. For example, I don't know anyone who made a Log Cabin quilt before the mid-1970's, although it was a much-admired pattern. Why? Because a thousand plus pieces individually marked, cut, and hand-sewn was too much for most of us. With the publication of efficient machine methods, however, it suddenly seemed that everyone made a Log Cabin. They were everywhere and they all looked similar. But that's okay: quilters were learning. After getting the method down, quilters began to play with the pattern, changing the number and width of strips, moving the center square off-center, introducing many fabrics for a scrap look, and even changing the shape of the block.

Each new method is like that. It is most meaningful to plug it into what we already know. Once we understand the mechanics of a method, we can progress to exploring the design potential of the method.

I believe the same thing will happen with, say, Equilateral Triangles (see page 127) and hexagon designs. Whether hand or machine piecing, it has always been difficult to set in the 120° angles of hexagons. As I said, the method used encourages or discourages the making of specific quilts. We don't see many hexagon quilts, other than Grandmother's Flower Garden. Yet I figured out a way to strip-piece and set hexagons row by row. Now that it's easy to machine-piece, I expect to see wonderful hexagon quilts in the years to come.

Some quilters don't like machine-piecing methods because so many look-alike quilts have been made using them—quilts without individuality, without

Each quilt in the book gives size, difficulty, time to make, yardage, and instructions on making and finishing. Some quilts are followed by Possibilities, alternatives meant to spark your creativity.

The margins in this book contain additional tips; comments, both historical and current; and quotes that have inspired me.

Some of us learn a method by reading instructions, some by looking at illustrations, and some by making samples or whole quilts. This is why all three have been included in this book. The goal of all three is to set you free.

When the bride brought the nicely browned turkey to the table, her husband asked why it was cut into two pieces. She replied that her mother had always done it that way. Later, he asked his mother-in-law why she cut her turkey in half. She said that her mother had always cut the turkey in half. When grandmother was asked the same question, she explained that her oven had been too small to hold the entire turkey.

The point is: We may be making the old quilt designs, but we are not in the same situation as the quiltmakers of a century or two ago. Our fabrics are relatively less costly. We often buy fabric specifically for making quilts. We have accurate means of measuring. Our sewing machines make sturdy, accurate seams.

The size of our stoves has changed and we no longer have to cut the turkey in half.

creativity, quilts that look like they were cranked out by a factory. I think so many cookie-cutter quilts have been made because for most quilters, it is a necessary first step in understanding the methods. I've always said that you can use these methods without understanding them and I constantly see additional proof of this. As quilters gain in understanding the methods, they will gain in seeing the potential of the methods. When this happens, they won't be satisfied with the narrow range of quilts being made today. I hope the day will come when only the greenest beginner will find comfort in an expensive book that tells her how to make one cookie-cutter quilt.

Because strip-piecing methods are so ordinary today, I've concentrated more in this book on Crystal Piecing. I believe it contains the potential for changing the look of quilts in the future. Remember, the construction method a quilter uses influences the quilts she is likely to make. If you are familiar with Strips and Strata and making such Crystal Piecing as Half-Square Triangles my way, go straight to Snowball (page 59), Equilateral Triangles (page 127), and Paired Quilts (page 139). But even for the more well-known techniques like Rail Fence, I've included Possibilities—ideas for new layouts of traditional blocks.

I've also included facsimiles of pages from my notebooks, for the truly adventuresome soul. I hope it gives you years of thought.

Simple Squares

Part One:

Understanding Quick Quiltmaking

"Mathematics is the alphabet with which God has written the universe. **"**
Galileo

Understanding Quick Quiltmaking

In the old days, quilters chose a quilt pattern, broke each block down into its components, and made a template for each component. Then they traced around each template on fabric and added seam allowances before cutting out the individual pieces and joining them by hand. This is called *template piecing*.

But there are two other faster ways to piece quilts.

As with template piecing, one method involves marking, cutting, and sewing. I call this method *Strips and Strata*. Here's one pattern of many.

If you are unfamiliar with the Strips and Strata methods of piecing quilts, see Chapter 6, page 82.

Template Piecing:
Mark/Cut/Sew

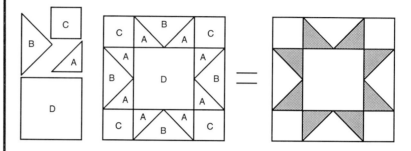

Strips and Strata:
Mark/Cut/Sew

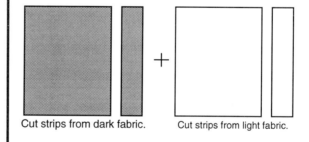

Cut strips from dark fabric.   Cut strips from light fabric.

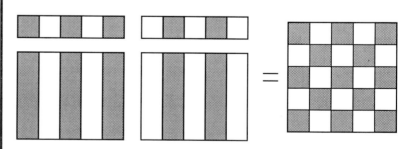

Sew strips together two ways into strata.
Cut across strata to form combinations.

Sew combinations
together to make quilt.

Crystal Piecing:

Mark/Sew/Cut

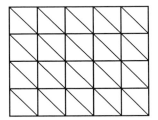 

Mark a square grid on the back of light-colored fabric. Mark parallel diagonal lines through every intersection.

Combine right sides together with another piece of fabric. Sew seam lines on each side of each parallel line.

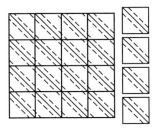 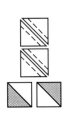 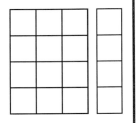

Cut the yardage apart on the grid lines into squares.

Cut each square on the center diagonal line into triangles. I call these combinations. Open the triangles up: you've made a square that's half light, half dark. I call this a Half-Square Triangle.

Now you need two sizes of plain squares for this quilt block. Cut strips of light-colored fabric the width of the squares (plus seam allowances). Slice across the strips to make squares.

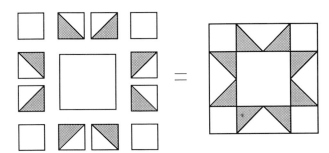

The second method of quick piecing involves a change in order of working: marking, sewing, then cutting. I call this method *Crystal Piecing*. Here's one pattern of many.

The end result looks exactly like that made in template piecing—except you have made enough combinations for the entire quilt, not just one block.

The concept of Crystal Piecing—Mark/Sew/Cut—can be applied in many exciting ways. That's the subject of this book.

I group both methods under the umbrella term *Quick Quiltmaking*.

1. ◆

Getting Started

Quick Quiltmaking allows you to piece whole quilt tops in hours instead of weeks. It does not, however, excuse you from being accurate or having high standards of workmanship.

Some Assumptions

When I started quilting, I worked in a virtual vacuum. We did not have, for example, the vast numbers of rulers now available. We didn't even have rotary cutters. These days we've all come a long way, but to be sure we're thinking on the same wavelength, here are my assumptions.

Yardage

All yardage quantities have been figured with 45" width fabric.

All patterns have been sized for 1/4" seams unless stated otherwise.

Workmanship

Saving time is not the ultimate goal: a beautiful quilt is. Do not be so concerned with saving time that you let the quality of your work suffer. Saving time is not an end in itself. Do not lose sight of quality workmanship.

Try to choose colors thoughtfully, to sew accurately, to match cross-seams precisely, to handle bias edges carefully, to machine quilt finely, and to bind your quilt appropriately. Then be proud.

Accuracy

The faster our tools, the faster we sew—but this does not ensure accuracy. Slow down when you're marking your fabric. It's here that accuracy now will save headaches later. Use the carpenter's advice: measure twice, cut once. Be sure your tools are accurate. Are you sure the grid on your cutting mat is accurate? Cheap ones may be off in one direction. Is your plastic ruler accurate? Not all of them are. Are the lines thick on your ruler? Then be sure you always use the same side of a line to measure and mark—i.e., right or left side. Otherwise the 1/16" you're off multiplied by the number of seams may make matching difficult. You could end up off 2" – 3".

Extras—Make More Than You Need

It is not realistic to think you will get every piece right the first time around. Sometimes you have to rip out your stitches, repin, and resew. Quick Quiltmaking methods being as fast as they are, it is easier to make extra components in the first place than it is to take apart the ones you have already made and resew them.

"Do what you can, with what you have, where you are."
Theodore Roosevelt

"Whenever I do quick triangles, I always have leftovers. I toss them into a box, along with other odd bits of strip sets, and then when I'm making a new piece of wearable art or a quick book cover for a teacher gift or Christmas present, I dip into this magic box for ready-made units."
Jennifer Amor, author
Flavor Quilts for Kids to Make
Columbia, SC

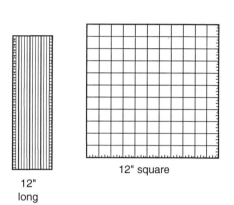

12"
long

12" square

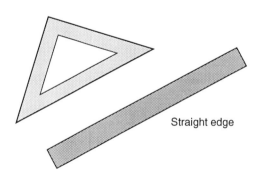

Straight edge

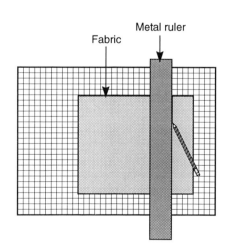

Fabric

Metal ruler

What counts is getting it right the final time and having the first time be the final time as often as possible.

If you find that one of your components is under- or oversized, toss it in the string-quilt or crazy-quilt scrap pile. I make about an extra 5% to allow for any that are not accurate. (Yardages in this book are calculated to account for the extra.)

Tools, Equipment, Material

When I originally wrote about my methods in the 1970's, there were no tools designed especially for machine piecing. We had to make do with general sewing supplies and items borrowed from the drafting field. The general sewing supplies were often not accurate enough for our needs and the drafting supplies were difficult to obtain.

Since that time, machine piecing has caught on. No longer do we wear the scarlet "M." The market has responded with many truly wonderful products that help us be faster, more efficient, and more accurate. (I must also say that there are many products of such limited usefulness that they are a waste of your money and the resources it took to make them—e.g., very few quilt patterns need their own specialized plastic tool.) Now we have the choice of several good ways of doing one task. Experiment until you find what tools that are most comfortable for you. In general, select tools that are versatile.

Basically you have your choice of

Two ways of measuring and marking:
1. With a grid and a straight edge, or
2. With one of the many specialized plastic rulers.

Two ways of cutting:
1. With scissors, or
2. With a rotary cutter and a cutting mat.

These can be combined in many ways to measure, mark, and cut fabric.

Measuring and Marking Methods

1. Grid and straight edge
In the 1970's, BT (before tools), I used a dressmaker's cutting board, warning of its many inherent shortcomings, like inaccurate markings and an annoying fold in the middle. Of course there was nothing else available at the time. I eventually gave mine to my son to play with.

Now I prefer a grid that is designed for architects and draftsmen. It is a heavy, plastic-coated paper grid and absolutely accurate, marked in 1/8" intervals. Grids come in different widths and are sold by the yard or fraction thereof. Look in the Yellow Pages under Architects' Supplies. Using a T-square, I lined my grid up square on my huge drafting table, then taped it down with a clear wide tape. My piece is 38" x 46". This allows for an entire yard of fabric to be marked at once. This grid allows for complete flexibility in its use, although very few quilters use a grid for marking, primarily due to its limited availability. Since it's a sea of 1/8" marks, the lines can be confusing. (I use Post-It Notes to mark the repeats.) Still, I love the absolute accuracy it gives me. I rarely have to worry about matching cross-seams, for example, because I was accurate from the beginning.

As for a straight edge, I use a metal yardstick or straight edge, available in hardware or art stores. Wooden yardsticks are often bowed, so check carefully for straightness. Those made of metal are more versatile because they can be used with rotary cutters. One shortcoming of metal straight edges is that they slip and slide on the fabric. Put masking tape or sand paper on one side to correct this potential problem. Finally try to locate a straight edge that is longer than 36". 39" or 40" works well. Having numbers on the yardstick is not necessary; in fact you generally should not use them. Instead, use the built-in accuracy of the grid.

I prefer marking with pencils, because the sharp tip provides a more accurate line. Venus Col-erase is one brand that has worked well for me. They are paper-erasable artist's drawing pencils. They come in a wide range of colors and so far have washed out completely.

Berol Prismacolor work well for sketching designs for just the opposite reasons. They lay down a thick, heavy layer of color.

2. Rulers

A variety of useful plastic tools have reached the market in the last few years. When choosing plastic rulers, select one with the greatest versatility. Choose one that will mark a variety of strip widths with one piece of plastic.

As always, check the individual ruler for accuracy before you use it. Buy a large one, such as 6" x 24". Consider how well the lines on the ruler will show up on both light and dark fabric. Does the ruler slide around or does it have a surface that helps it grab the fabric?

Warning: Although I use this grid, I don't advocate it for most people because it's not an easy tool to use.

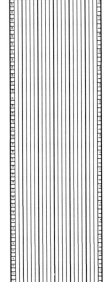

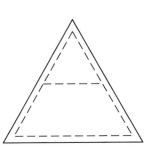

Warning: Plastic tools have depth and the lines are printed on only one side. The line will seem to be where it isn't, so your measurements can be inaccurate. Use rulers with the printed lines down, against the fabric.

Generally, I prefer "vague" tools, so I do not buy specialty rulers invented for one purpose. Exceptions are specialty rulers cut to 60° angles. They will make the marking of diamonds and equilateral triangles, such as Spider Web, much easier. If you can't afford a special ruler, you can mark these lines with a rectangular ruler with 60° lines marked. If the ruler has the 60° lines going in both directions, you won't have to keep flipping it over. Happily, there are many types to choose from.

Cutting Methods

1. Scissors

You can, of course, use one pair of scissors for everything, but specialized scissors give such superior results that their cost is well worth it. I learned the importance of good tools many years ago. We had only one pair of scissors in the house. They were used for everything. They did an okay job of cutting paper, plastic, cardboard, etc., but tended to chew fabric rather than cutting it.

The first time I tried Ginghers, it was a revelation. They could slice through as many as eight layers of fabric with less effort than my former scissors could chew through one. Furthermore, I have a left-handed pair—a pure sensual delight after struggling for years with right-handed scissors. I realized how important good tools are to both your enjoyment in sewing and the end results. So if you use 100% cotton fabric, use a pair of scissors like Ginghers, and use them only on 100% cotton, so as not to damage the blades on something else. Sharpen as needed. These are a joy to work with. Tie a piece of yarn or whatever on them, so everyone knows which scissors they must never use. Use another pair of scissors for cutting cotton/polyester fabric and polyester batts. Also a pair of thread snippers is handy. Finally, you can buy quite adequate paper scissors for just a few dollars. Have several pairs placed around the house for anyone to use on whatever they want.

2. Rotary cutter and mat

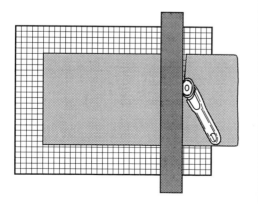

Rotary cutters look like pizza cutters designed to cut fabric. They seem to have been designed with machine-piecing methods in mind, especially for Strips and Strata. They can cut through several layers at once, as well as allowing you to bypass some marking, as you cut along the edge of the straight edge or plastic ruler. Always make sure the guard covers the blade after *each* use. (BE CAREFUL: Improper use of rotary cutters can result in severe cuts to you.) Buy a large cutter and replace the blade as needed. Hold it so that the blade is perpendicular to the ruler, rather than angled in to the fabric. Always roll away from your body. Never place your fingers in the pathway of the blade. This is a powerful tool that can greatly speed up your work. Respect it.

If you use a rotary cutter, you will need a good cutting mat. It is the surface that the blade connects with after it cuts through your fabric and before it cuts through your table. Many sizes and shapes are available. Most commonly available are cutting mats with grids on them. The grid lines are thick, which can lead to inaccurate cutting. Get in the habit of always aligning the ruler with the center of the line or the right side or the top edge of the lines. A bumpy surface will help your fabric stay put rather than slide and shift. Finally, buy the largest mat you can afford and have room for.

Fabric

Most people prefer to use 100% cotton. Cotton shrinks. That raises a question.

Prewashing Fabric

To prewash or not to prewash? That is the question. The answer is: it all depends. You will have to decide for yourself.

The basic purpose of prewashing is to remove the possibility of surprises when the quilt is washed after it is made.

I buy good-quality fabric and have rarely had a problem with the dye. I generally prewash, but others never do and are happy with the results. You decide.

Sewing and Pressing

All the marking and cutting accuracy in the world is destroyed if you don't sew an accurate seam allowance and press carefully.

Seam allowance guides

When you sew strips, you get the machine going as fast as it will go. For this reason the short markings on the needleplate will not do as a guide. You need a guide to help you sew the proper seam width. The guide should be one seam width from the needle and it should be long. You can buy attachments that serve this function. They physically guide the fabric at the proper seam width. A 4"-long piece of tape also works well. If you use several layers of tape, you will get a physical as well as a visual guide. (If you layer the tape, you must remove it to change seam widths.) Generally, no seam lines are marked when doing strip piecing. Rather, you ignore the needle and watch the fabric edge, always keeping it even with

Recommendations

Spend your money first on quality scissors, a rotary cutter, a long metal yardstick, a big cutting mat, and a big versatile plastic ruler. These will produce the greatest results at the cheapest cost. Add the new sewing machine when you can afford it.

Prewash

Shrinks fabric 1-3%

Gets rid of excess dye

Determines if the dye is set

Removes sizing

Removes chemicals

Determines the permanency of a specific finish

Prevents surprises after your quilt is finished

No Prewash

Less work

Few good quality fabrics lose dye or shrink excessively

The stiffness of the fabric caused by the sizing actually makes the fabric easier to work with in machine methods.

If you machine quilt using a cotton batt and wash the quilt when you finish, the fabric and the batt will shrink together, rather than the cotton batt shrinking inside the already preshrunk quilt.

All the quilts in my first books were calculated with 1/2" seam allowances. This was because my students wanted practicality in quilts. They wanted a quilt durable enough to withstand rough-housing kids wearing shoes. I had seen many old quilts whose 1/4" seams had frayed out from the inside. I came up with a pieced top of durable kettlecloth sewn with equally durable 1/2" seams, and quilted or tied. Additionally, the 1/2" seams made the math easy.

Then the quilt revolution of the mid-70's occurred. The new quilters were more interested in quiltmaking as a creative expression than as a way to create practical bedcoverings. A controversy developed over my use of 1/2" seam allowances, which detracted from the acceptance of machine-piecing methods. Quilters seemed to reason: "You have to use 1/2" seam allowances in machine piecing. We use 1/4" seam allowances. Therefore, the new method is no good. We'll stick to templates and handpiecing."

Using 1/2" seam allowances was my biggest self-created stumbling block to the acceptance of machine piecing.

Ironically, a quilting teacher recently told me that she still uses 1/2" seam allowances with beginners. "It's easier for them," she says.

the tape. Some sewing machine feet are 1/4" wide, but even so, I like a long guide.

Seam allowances

Match your seam allowance to what you are sewing.

1/4" seams for:

Work that will be hand-quilted.

Any quilt that will be quilted extensively.

All small-scale piecing, including anything less than 3".

1/2" seams for:

Anything that will be tied and used heavily.

The edges of minimally secured piecing (1/4" or less) can fray from the inside. On some quilts with 1/4" seams, you may want to allow for a 1/2" seam on the outside edge of the outer blocks. This gives you a little fudge factor in matching blocks. Or make more blocks than are required and leave out those that are off-size.

Pressing pointers

Always press gently. Never stretch the fabric. Pressing is an up-and-down motion. Let the weight of the iron press the fabric rather than the strength of your arm. Forceful pressing can stretch accurate piecing out of shape. Be especially careful when pressing bias fabric.

Lay the sewn strips on the board, dark fabric on top, wrong side up. Open the top fabric up and press the seam from the top side. This presses the seam

toward the dark fabric (reverse if you want seams pressed toward the light). When pressing on the top side, it is easy to make sure the piece is opened completely.

Accurate marking, cutting, and sewing are useless unless the piecing is pressed open completely. While I use an iron to press, there are others who believe that only finger pressing should be used until the block is complete.

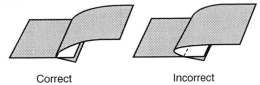

Correct   Incorrect

The Three Musts of Pressing

1. Press your fabric before marking it.

2. Press seam allowances either to one side, generally toward the darker fabric, or open (see below).

3. Always press before crossing a seam with another piece.

Pattern permitting, press so that one set of seam allowances goes one way and the other set goes the other way. This creates less bulk.

When joining blocks or rows, does your sewing machine grab the bottom fabric and push away the top fabric? If it does, pattern permitting, press so that the top seam allowances face the sewing machine needle and the bottom seam allowances face away from the needle. The ridges caused by the pressing lock together for a perfect cross-match.

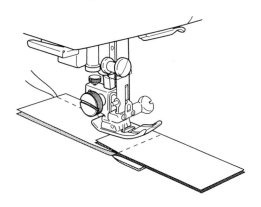

About sewing machines: I made my first pieced top on Grandma Ida's 1906 White treadle. Then I used Mom's 1946 Kenmore for my first strip-pieced quilt. Today I work on a Kenmore portable bought in the 1970's. While I'd like a newer machine, I think working with ordinary machines in the beginning forced me to be more attentive and inventive with the methods. You can do a lot with the basics.

Tip Deb Wagner, author of *Teach Yourself Machine Piecing and Quilting*, recommends starching fabric heavily before cutting it. It doesn't ripple under a rotary cutter or get eaten by the sewing machine.

My editor has recently convinced me that pressing seams open is a good idea. It's easier to match crossing seams.

Press to one side:

◆ If the seam allowance will show through one of your fabrics

◆ If you will be machine quilting using Stitch-in-the-Ditch

Press open:

◆ If you want easier matching of cross seams

◆ If you won't be using Stitch-in-the-Ditch

Terms

We need names for our fabric at each stage of construction, so we can be sure we are all talking about the same thing. We start with strips and strip piecing from Seminole techniques. After that, we need to agree on some new names. Some of the terms I've come up with have caught on and some have not. Others have come up with good names. Where a name has not been decided on by common usage, I have listed the variations I have heard.

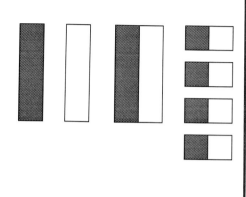

Strips

The result of marking and cutting yardage into long narrow pieces

Strata

Strips sewn together along their long sides, making a fabric from which combinations of squares, rectangles, diamonds, or other shapes are cut. Also called panels or bands.

Half-Square Triangles

Result of dividing a square diagonally. In Crystal Piecing, they are made in pairs, sewn together along their *long sides*.

Quarter-Square Triangles

Result of dividing a square diagonally in both directions. In Crystal Piecing, they are made in pairs, sewn together along two of their *short sides*. Geometrically, Half-Square Triangles and Quarter-Square Triangles are the same. The difference is on which side they are sewn together.

Crystal Piecing

Refers to the process and product of marking a piece of fabric, placing it with an unmarked piece, sewing them together, and then cutting them apart into combinations. Half-Square and Quarter-Square Triangles are two of many geometric shapes that can be made with this method. Originally, I called this method tandem piecing, which fits. Others called it sandwich piecing, which also fits. Now I'm calling it Crystal Piecing, because of the incredible unexplored potential of the method. The resulting units can be composed of many pieces of fabric and can look like jewels.

Combinations

The pieces resulting when Crystal Piecing or Strata is cut. When the resulting piece is composed of two pieces of fabric, it is often called a pair.

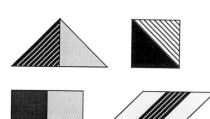

Floating in the Third Dimension

Part Two:

Crystal Piecing

The following sections give exact instructions for constructing 8 quilt tops. Finishing instructions are in Part Four: Machine Quilting.

Since many of these techniques are brand-new, I also show you Possibilities. I hope you will experiment, discover, expand the quilting repertoire.

Once you have mastered the Crystal Piecing basics, see Part Five: Design Your Own Quilt for ideas on original design.

2.

Crystal Piecing: Mark/Sew/Cut

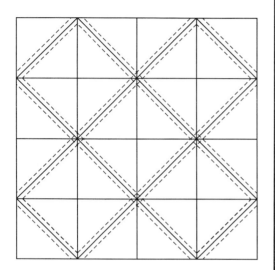

By now, most quilters commonly use the Strips and Strata method of quick-piecing patterns. This initially involves marking the fabric, cutting strips, and sewing them into strata. The strata is then cut at various angles to make combinations, which are combined with other shapes and sewn together to make blocks or quilt tops. See Part Three for a description of Strips and Strata methods, including some little-explored shapes like equilateral triangles.

But a second way to quick-piece patterns has been barely explored. I call this method Crystal Piecing, a name that conveys its incredible potential. Crystal Piecing involves marking the top fabric of two layers, sewing them together, and cutting them apart into combinations. The results can look like jewels. Notice the change in order of working from Strips and Strata: mark/**sew**/cut. That is the key to a wide range of amazing shapes.

Experienced quilters are familiar with the Crystal Piecing that produces Half-Square Triangles. Some know how to construct Quarter-Square Triangles with Crystal Piecing. But so much more is possible. After you mark, sew, and cut, you can come up with more than two units sewn together—you can have three, four, five, or more.

And the combinations are not limited to squares. After all, does anyone still think that strip piecing means sewing together only two strips from which we cut only squares? Of course not! We cut rectangles, diamonds, even equilateral triangles, often from more than two strips.

Why not apply the same thinking to Crystal Piecing? I will show you how to mark a square grid, sew across it on the diagonal, and cut to produce squares or 90° triangles. But what if we mark rectangles? What if we sew on the grid lines instead of the diagonals?

The resulting shapes are different from traditional ones. This is the magic of Crystal Piecing and I expect great things of it. Those much more talented than I am at designing will use Crystal Piecing to design new types of quilts, both traditional and contemporary, never seen before.

The construction method a quilter uses shapes both the types of quilts she makes and the final design. Exploring the potential of Crystal Piecing will change the designs of quilts in the 1990's just as strip piecing changed the quilting world in the 1970's. I can hardly wait to see what you do with it.

When you divide a square diagonally, the two resulting shapes are called Half-Square Triangles, the most common type of triangle used in piecing. They can be put together in a limitless variety of traditional and original patterns.

Half-Square Triangles usually occur in pairs. When they do, it's a signal to mass-produce and speed-piece them with the following method. You will mark one piece of fabric, sew it to the second, and finally cut out the already-pieced triangle combinations. Instead of methodically marking, cutting, and sewing single triangles, as with template piecing, in Crystal Piecing you mark lengths of yardage at a time and piece nearly all your Half-Square Triangles at once.

This method is not only fast, but, just as important, with it you sew on the fabric before it has been cut on the bias, minimizing stretching.

If you are unfamiliar with Half-Square Triangles, read through the instructions. Then practice on scraps of fabric before plunging in on the project you have in mind.

3.◆
Half-Square Triangles

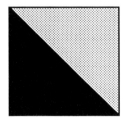

> By joining two large units of fabric before cutting, joining bias seams is eliminated. I consider this the greatest contribution that Barbara has made to advance the techniques of quilting.
>
> My own work seldom contains much colour repetition in Half-Square Triangles. But even when doing one-of-a-kind things, I use Barbara's techniques all the time. It makes the whole procedure more efficient and accurate, and allows me to spend my energy on making the colour movement in the design beautiful, because I know the piecing will be accurate. "

Pat Cairns, author
*Contemporary Quilting Techniques/
A Modular Approach*
Vancouver, BC, Canada

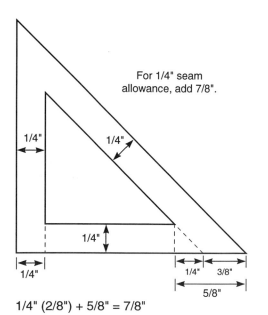

For 1/4" seam allowance, add 7/8".

1/4" (2/8") + 5/8" = 7/8"

Determining the Marking Size

In the Strips and Strata method, we calculate the cutting size of squares by adding two times the seam allowance to the finished size. A square that finishes 3" with 1/4" seam allowances would be cut from 3-1/2" strips.

But Half-Square Triangles are different. To allow for the 1/4" seam allowances on the diagonal of the square, you must add 7/8" to the finished size of the final square you want, not 1/2", as with squares.

You must understand the difference between the marking size and the finished size. It may not be what you think it is.

1. Decide on the finished size of the squares.
2. Add on the Half-Square Triangle seam allowance.

Finished Size of Square	Marking Interval
2"	2-7/8"
2-1/8"	3"
3"	3-7/8"
3-1/8"	4"

This number, 7/8", can be awkward to mark across the yardage. We aren't used to marking in intervals of eighths, yet we usually design blocks to finish as whole numbers—e.g., a 9" block might have three 3" squares in each row, two of which might be Half-Square Triangles. For the Half-Square Triangles to finish 3", we'd have to mark a 3-7/8" grid both ways across the yardage.

After I show you the principles of making Half-Square Triangles, I'll suggest ways to deal with eighths.

This method is most easily done with a large, general-purpose plastic see-through ruler. First we'll mark a grid for the cutting lines. Then we'll mark diagonal sewing lines.

John Flynn, *King's X*, 96" x 108". This is John's interpretation of Johannah's *Governor's Palace Maze* with his braided border around it.

Judy Speller, *Star of Bethlehem,* 96″ x 192″, a much-loved quilt owned by Judy's son

Designed by Barbara Johannah, made by Sharon Hose, *Grandmother's Flower Garden,* 59″ x 72″. These shapes are strip-pieced, then cut into equilateral triangles and pieced horizontally. The final design is a hexagon (see Chapter 10).

Warren Whaley, *Woven Squares*, 83" x 92½"

Warren Whaley, *Medallion*, 85" x 172"

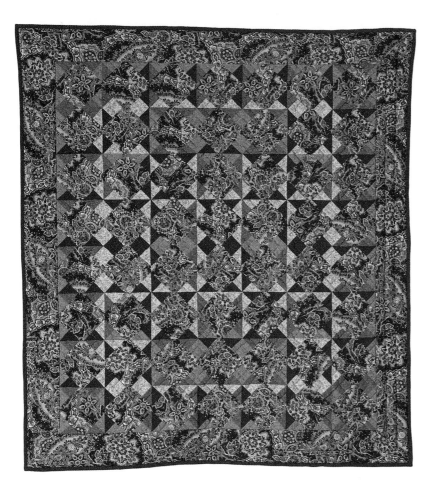

Pat Whittemore, *Garnet II,* 24" x 31½" (see Chapter 5).

Carla Rodio, *Four Seasons,* 48" square;
© 1991 Rodio

Sharon Hose, *Tulip*, 13¾" x 41½". Strip-pieced, cut into equilateral triangles, and pieced horizontally; Continuous Curve Quilting.

Pat Whittemore, *Garnet I*, 24" x 31½" (see Chapter 5).

Jane Warnick. Quilt designs (see elsewhere in color section) done for her grandchildren, Colin and Lisa, were developed from birthdates matched to the Half-Square Triangle Element Key (see pages 186–187).

Charlotte Patera, *Amish Molas*,
24" x 28"

Barbara Johannah, *Sapphire*, 27½"
square. Strip-pieced, then paired
with plain yardage and Crystal-
Pieced into Half-Square Triangles
(see Chapter 5).

Constructing the Triangles

1. For this demonstration, use light and dark fabrics the size of a fat half (18" x 21"). Determine what size finished square you want. In this example, using a 1/4" seam allowance, you'll mark at 3-7/8" intervals and finish at 3". Of the two pieces of fabric you will be using, mark the wrong side of the lighter fabric.

2. Angling the pencil in toward the ruler, mark five lines vertically and horizontally at 3-7/8" intervals. These will eventually be your cutting lines.

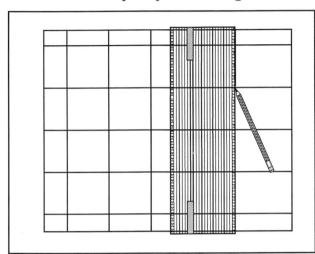

3. Now mark the triangles. These too will eventually be cutting lines. Draw a diagonal line through every other square in one direction. Draw diagonal lines in all other squares in the opposite direction.

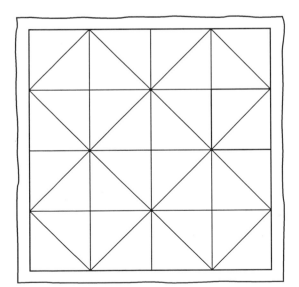

Tip You can save yourself a lot of aggravation caused by mismarking if you premark the ruler with tape. Near each end, place small pieces of tape at the 3-7/8" line. An easily removable tape like Post-It Notes works well for a few triangles; use masking tape for marking many triangles.

Tape

3-7/8"

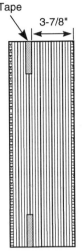

I originally marked all the squares with parallel diagonal lines (see page X), but I like this method developed by Marti Michell and Linda Turner Griepentrog better.

4. Next mark sewing lines rather than cutting lines. (You may want to use a different color of pencil.) Mark 1/4" on each side of the diagonal lines. Follow the marking pattern in the diagram for the greatest ease in sewing.

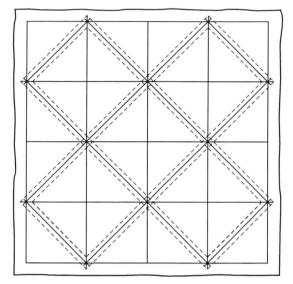

5. Place the piece you have just marked on top of your contrasting fabric, right sides together. Pin in each triangle as shown. This is to hold the fabric together and keep it from shifting while it is being sewn.

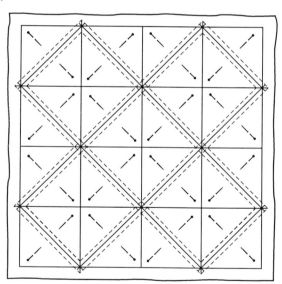

6. Sew only on the parallel diagonal *stitching* lines. When you reach the edge of the fabric, pivot 90° and stitch the next line. Remove the pins from the fabric now if you did not do so while you were sewing.

7. Cut on the horizontal and vertical grid lines. You're cutting out squares. Then cut each square in half between the diagonal stitching lines. Remove the few stitches at the tips of each triangle.

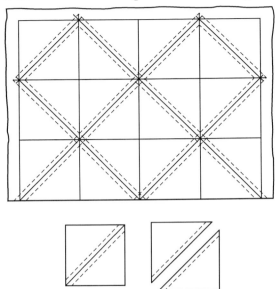

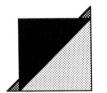

8. Open triangles and press seams toward the darker fabric (or open, if you prefer). Trim the ears of the seam allowance sticking out beyond the edges. You now have a stack of pre-made Half-Square Triangle combinations. They are now ready to make up into whatever pattern you have in mind.

Anything But Eighths

Over the years since my first book was published, the only method a significant number of people have had any trouble with is marking Half-Square Triangles. Perhaps they should be called Troublesome Triangles instead. Some of the problem came originally from the lack of tools.

When using 1/4" seams, the marking size of the square is 7/8" larger than the finished size. It's not an easy number to measure and mark across yardage. But that doesn't mean you can't work around it so you don't have to mark successive 7/8's inches. There are many ways, some useful, some Rube Goldberg-ish. Here are their pro's and con's.

The Quick Quiltmaking Handbook was ahead of its time. Think what Barbara could have done if rotary cutting equipment had been available.

Lassie Wittman
Rochester, WA

Chapter 3. **Half-Square Triangles** | **29**

Finished Size of Square	Marking Interval
2"	2-7/8"
2-1/8"	3"
3"	3-7/8"
3-1/8"	4"

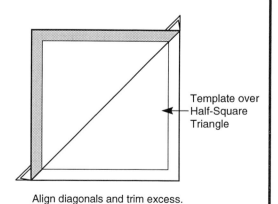

Template over
Half-Square
Triangle

Align diagonals and trim excess.

A. Use a plastic ruler. Avoid using the grid/straight edge to mark your fabric into triangles. It is the successive addition of 7/8's that makes marking in eighths difficult. I originally developed the method for making triangles before appropriate tools existed. Now the market has responded to the development of the methods by providing many good plastic see-through rulers. You can mark the cutting size on the ruler rather than on the grid. (See page 17).

B. Mark in whole inches and finish in fractions. Start by working backward on the chart. Choose an easy marking interval. For example, mark 4" and finish sewing with 3-1/8" squares. This is the obvious choice when all or most of the pieces will be Half-Square Triangles. You're always marking in whole inches. The Double Four Patch and Ocean Wave quilts fit in this category (see pages 35 and 43).

C. Use a 1/2" seam allowance. Instead of adding 7/8" to the finished size, add 1-3/4". It doesn't make it any easier marking across a grid, but somehow it feels easier to mark a plastic ruler at the 3/4" mark than the 7/8" mark. Using a larger seam allowance uses more fabric, but not an excessive amount.

D. Sew a fat 1/4" seam. Mark in whole inches, which leaves an extra 1/8" to work into the two diagonal seam lines (1" - 7/8" = 1/8"). If you sew slightly wider than 1/4" on the diagonal—i.e., a fat 1/4"—it will take up the slack. For example, mark 4", sew a fat 1/4" seam allowance and hope you finish at 3". Just exactly how wide is a fat 1/4"? The answer is 23/64". You may be able to decenter the needle on your machine to achieve this, but most of us aren't that accurate. If you want the Half-Square Triangles to finish an accurate measurement, the lack of precision in this approach won't do.

E. Change the measurement. Do as Pat Cairns does and mark your squares 1-1/2" larger than the finished size. Sew a 1/4" diagonal seam and cut out as usual. Make a plastic template of the finished square with a diagonal line on it. Align the seam line on each Half-Square Triangle with the template, matching diagonal lines. You can center the template or put it in one corner. Trim all around. The trimming creates an extra step, but the marking is easy.

F. Mark in inches and use the Equalizer. What's an Equalizer? A tool I invented that marks a precise fat 1/4". I'll draw it for you here and you can copy it onto plastic template material. Mark the squares 1" larger than finished size, rather than 7/8". Then use the Equalizer to mark the diagonal sewing lines. It will take up that difficult-to-deal-with 1/8". Turn the Equalizer over so that the line is underneath. Place it so that the center line diagonally bisects the corners of the squares. Mark on each side of the Equalizer, using a reasonably sharp pencil. You've now marked a precise seam.

G. Don't use my method at all. Here are two alternatives.

◆ Sew light and dark strips together. Using the seam line as the diagonal of the Half-Square Triangle, use a square template to cut out squares. As you can see, this wastes material at the sides.

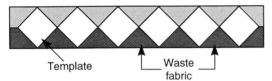

Template   Waste fabric

Also, if you sew straight-grain strips together, after cutting, your squares will have all four sides on the bias. If you want the squares' sides to be on grain, your strips have to be cut and sewn on the bias. You can avoid that by cutting bias strips and sewing them together. Either way you're handling bias, which easily stretches out of shape.

Cons: Wastes time and fabric and you have to deal with bias edges.

◆ Make a template to mark triangles and cut them from a strip. For example, to get a triangle with a 2" base, make 2-1/2" wide strips. Draw around a 2"-base triangle template. Flip it to the other side of the strip and move the base 3/4" away from the first triangle. Continue marking the strip this way. Then sew on the diagonal lines. Cut between them. Cut on the shared vertical line between triangles.

Cons: If you have to go to the trouble of measuring the 3/4" and 2-1/2" intervals, you might as well mark whole cloth.

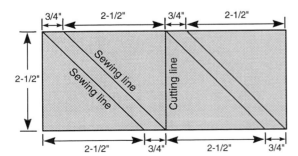

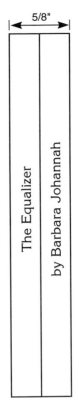

5/8"

The Equalizer
by Barbara Johannah

Make tool whatever length you prefer — 12" - 15"

The Equalizer
by Barbara Johannah

✎ In my first books, I gave people an alternative of using either 1/4" or 1/2" seam allowances and gave the measurements for both. (See explanation on page 20.) I took more flak for using 1/2" seam allowances than for my radical methods.

Chapter 3. **Half-Square Triangles** | **31**

All of these additional ways of marking Half-Square Triangles demonstrate our ability to achieve the desired result in many ways, as well as our aversion to working with eighths.

If you will be making your entire quilt from the same size of Half-Square Triangles, I suggest you mark in whole inches and finish in fractions.

If you will be combining other shapes with Half-Square Triangles in your quilt—squares, for example—make your decision based on what would be the easiest to do. Is it easier to mark in whole inches for the triangles, finish in fractions, and measure the strips to cut the squares in fractions? Or is it easier to plan your block size and quilt top in finished whole sizes—12", for example—thus demanding you mark Half-Square Triangles in fractions and finish in whole inches?

Half-Square Triangles: Medallion

This is a good first project if you've never made Half-Square Triangles before. It's also a welcome new-baby gift that doesn't take too long to make.

Because we are combining Half-Square Triangles with squares and rectangles, it's easier to measure in fractions and finish in whole inches.

Baby Quilt or Wallhanging, 40" x 40"
Time—fast
Difficulty—easy

Yardage

Quilt top:
   1-1/4 yards solid fabric
   1-1/4 yards print fabric
Backing: 1-1/4 yards
Recommended batting: See page 179.

Seam allowance: 1/4"

Finished size of square: 4"

Marking size of grid: 4-7/8"

Width of strips for squares: 4-1/2"

Combinations needed:
    68 Half-Square Triangles

Tip You could cut two rectangles, 4-1/2" x 16-1/2" and two rectangles, 4-1/2" x 24-1/2" and not piece squares at the ends of the inner side pieces (see assembly diagram). I like the look of the seam lines, so I pieced squares instead.

Making the Quilt Top

1. From the width, cut two strips 4-1/2" wide from the print fabric. Then cut 12 squares from the strips. Cut two 4-1/2" wide strips from the solid fabric and set aside.

2. Following the general instructions for Half-Square Triangles on page 25, make at least 68 combinations from the remaining print and solid fabric. Mark the grid at 4-7/8" intervals on the back of the solid fabric. Press seam allowances away from the light fabric.

3. Piece the center medallion, studying the assembly diagram. First join the triangle combinations into rows, then join the rows. Press seam allowances to one side. Piece the two outside rows at the sides, top, and bottom, but do not join yet.

4. Measure pieced panels before cutting these pieces from the solid-colored strips:

four squares, 4-1/2" x 4-1/2"

four rectangles, 4-1/2" x 16-1/2"

5. Following the assembly diagram, piece the three top bands and the three bottom bands to the center medallion. Then piece the two sides.

Finishing

Use the Envelope Method on page X. This quilt is easily machine-quilted with Continuo179s Curve Quilting following the directions on pages 174.

See Part Four: Machine Quilting for more information.

Barbara Johannah's Crystal Piecing

Quilt designed by Jennifer Amor

Half-Square Triangles: Double Four Patch

Double Four Patches are so easily made and so incredibly versatile. Each block is made from 16 Half-Square Triangle combinations. By turning the combinations in different directions, multiple patterns are created.

Because the blocks use only Half-Square Triangles, without adding additional squares, we will measure in whole inches and finish in fractions.

Queen, 90" x 106"
Time—average
Difficulty—average

Yardage

Quilt top:

3-1/2 yards of dark fabric

3-1/2 yards of light fabric

3-3/4 yards for lattice and borders* (see page 36)

Backing: 7 yards

Recommended batting: See page 179.

Seam allowance: 1/4"

Finished size of Half-Square Triangle Combinations: 3-1/8"

Marking size of grid: 4"

Finished size of block: 12-1/2"

Number of blocks: 20

Width of lattice: 3-1/8"

Width of border*: 6-1/4"

Combinations needed: 520 Half-Square Triangles

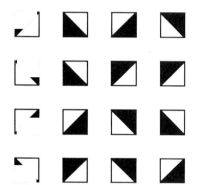

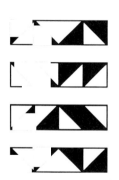

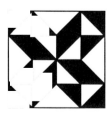

Barbara Fritchie Star

Making the Quilt Top

1. Don't let all of the following measurements throw you. They are for reference. Just cut the pieces the right width and plenty long. After they are sewn on, trim to fit.

Border—Cut:

two 7" x 93" along top (approximate finished size is 6-1/4" x 90-5/8")

two 7" x 96" along side (approximate finished size is 6-1/4" x 93-6/8")

* If you cut the border pieces 1-1/2" wider than the size given, you can turn them to the back and use as the binding (not included in yardage figure).

Lattice Strips—Cut:

two 3-5/8" x 78" along side (approximate finished size is 3-1/8" x 75")

two 3-5/8" x 68" along top (approximate finished size is 3-1/8" x 65-5/8")

four 3-5/8" x 62" (approximate finished size is 3-1/8" x 59-3/8")

fifteen 3-5/8" x 14" (approximate finished size is 3-1/8" x 12-1/2")

2. Refer to general instructions for making Half-Square Triangles on page 25. Make 520 Half-Square Triangle combinations following the general instructions. Mark your lines an even 4" apart. When a 1/4" seam is taken on all four sides of the Half Square Triangle combinations, they should finish 3-1/8".

3. Sew 16 Half-Square Triangles together to make one block. Join Half-Square Triangle combinations into rows. Join rows into completed blocks. Suggestions for block designs are given in the quilt on page 35, with additional possibilities on page 39. You could make the quilt all of one pattern or mix patterns.

The block used here is the Barbara Fritchie Star. It is in the four corners of the quilt. I understand that the block was designed in her honor. "Shoot if you must this old gray head, but spare my country's flag, she said" was the bit of verse which inspired this pattern. I could not resist the block nor the sentiment.

4. Make 20 blocks. Lay out the design on your floor or bed top. You can follow the quilt design on page 35 or design your own. Join blocks with a short strip of lattice in between. Trim excess lattice after seaming. Press seams to one side or open. After joining each row, return it to the bed or floor in position.

5. Sew the 62" lattice strips between rows, pressing after each seam. Trim excess lattice. Sew the 68" lattice strips to the sides. Trim excess. Sew the remaining 78" lattice strips to the top and bottom. Trim and press.

6. Construct the pieced border of the remaining Half-Square Triangle combinations. Make two strips of 13 diamonds. Make four strips of six diamonds each.

7. Sew the longer strips of diamonds to the two sides of the quilt. Lay the shorter strips on the top and bottom of the quilt and measure the gap in the middle. No dimensions are given for the fill-in pieces that go in the middle of the pieced borders. Each person produces a different size of combination. Cut whatever size joining piece you need to make the border the correct length. Having a break in the piecing design makes the border easier to fit.

8. Add the last border, sewing the side pieces first, then the top and bottom.

Finishing

If you have cut the last borders wider, you can layer and baste the quilt in the traditional way (see page 180), and turn the border to the back to use as a binding.

Due to the visual complexity caused by the use of so many blocks, Ernest Haight's Machine Quilting Method wouldn't be suitable. Continuous Curve Quilting with some possible Stitch-in-the-Ditch would be an appropriate choice. See Part Four: Machine Quilting for more information.

"The Double Four-Patch Sampler was one of the first classes I taught and it was wildly successful. Students made this quilt in everything from crib size to king-size waterbed. The great thing was that even beginners could create a complicated design with very little effort. Every quilt was different, but the technique remained the same. The design possibilities are endless. Students who would go into shock if you told them to design their own quilt suddenly find that by turning their Half-Square Triangles around, they can create something new and wonderful."

Jennifer Amor, author
Flavor Quilts for Kids to Make
Columbia, SC

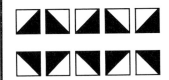

Half-Square Triangles become border.

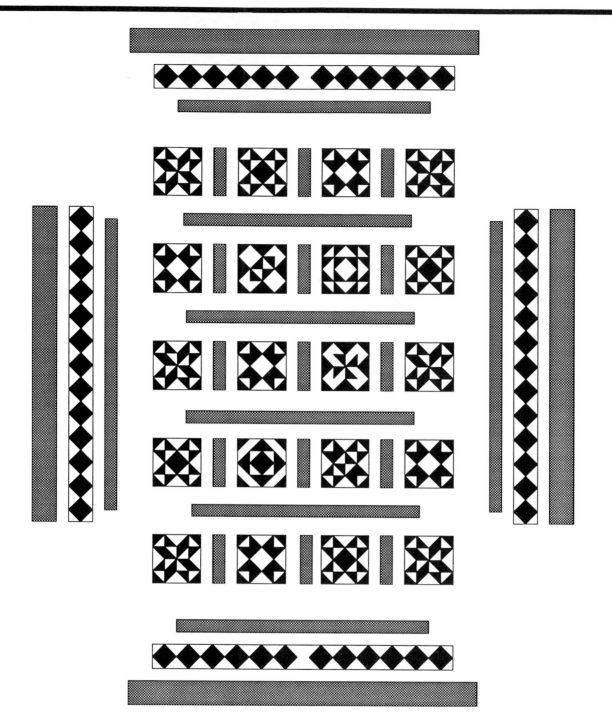

There are many collections of traditional quilt patterns. I often use Judy Rehmel's many Key books (e.g., *Key to 1000 Quilt Patterns*) for reference. Experiment to see if you can design additional blocks. In this blank Double Four Patch grid, simply color in half of each square.

Here are some possibilities.

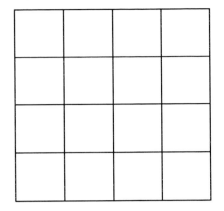

Half-Square Triangles: 25-Patch Sampler

I often used this 25-Patch Sampler as a class project for beginning quilters. Kyoko Akao designed the border for her sampler quilt.

The entire quilt is made from squares, rectangles and Half-Square Triangles. None of the blocks are difficult, but you are doing 12 different ones, so take extra care when making the blocks.

Note that Half-Square Triangle combinations are made from both background/medium fabric and from background/dark fabric.

Not all the pieces of the blocks can be made with Crystal Piecing. Some will be individually cut and pieced.

Twin or Double, 75" x 93"
Time—average
Difficulty—average

Yardage

Quilt top:
  3-5/8 yards background (light) fabric
  2 yards medium fabric
  4-1/4 yards dark fabric
Backing: 5-1/2 yards
Binding: 1-1/4 yards
Recommended batting: See page 179.

Making the Quilt Top

Pieces Needed for the Blocks

	Shape/Size	Background	Medium	Dark
1. Triangle Combinations Make Half-Square Triangle combinations following the general instructions. Mark at 3-7/8" intervals.	◿	← 191 combinations →		
		← 143 combinations →		
2. Square Combinations Make these by following the general instructions for working with strips and strata. The strips should be 3-1/2" wide and 25" long. You will need two dark strips and one background fabric strip.	(strip)	← 6 combinations →		
3. Individual Pieces Mark and cut out the individual pieces in the sizes indicated.	3-1/2" x 3-1/2"	15	12	20
	3-1/2" x 6-1/2"	16	8	4
	9-1/2" / 9-1/2" (triangle)		2	2
	6-1/2" / 6-1/2" (triangle)		1	1
	3-1/2" x 9-1/2"		5	

4. Lattice strips and border: Put aside the fabric reserved for the lattice strips and border until the blocks are completed. Measure the blocks and then adjust the size of the lattice strips and border accordingly if necessary.

Cut from your fabric: 2 3-1/2" x 87-1/2"   5 3-1/2" x 51-1/2"
                       4 3-1/2" x 75-1/2"   8 3-1/2" x 15-1/2"

Seam allowance: 1/4"

Finished size of squares: 3"

Marking size of grid: 3-7/8"

Finished size of blocks: 15"

Number of blocks: 12

Width of lattice: 3"

Width of border: 3"

Combinations needed:
191 Half-Square Triangle combinations of background/medium
143 combinations of background/dark
6 Square combinations of dark/background/dark

1. Measure about 90" along the lengthwise grain of the dark fabric and cut across. Then cut the following lengthwise strips for lattice and borders:

two 3-1/2" x 87-1/2"

four 3-1/2" x 75-1/2"

five 3-1/2" x 51-1/2"

eight 3-1/2" x 15-1/2"

2. Cut 2-1/8 yards each from dark and background fabric. Cut 1-2/3 yards each from medium and background fabric. Marking a 3-7/8" grid on the background fabric, make 143 Half-Square Triangle combinations for background/dark and 191 for background/medium, following the general instructions on page 25.

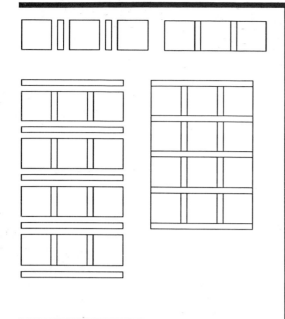

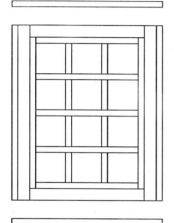

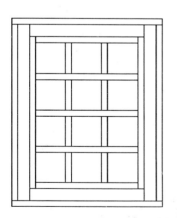

3. Square Combinations: Make these by following the general instructions for working with Strips and Strata on page 82. The strips should be 3-1/2" wide and 25" long. You will need two dark strips and one background fabric strip. Later you will slice across these combinations so they are 3-1/2" wide.

4. Mark and cut out individual pieces in the sizes indicated below:

	Background	Medium	Dark
3-1/2" x 3-1/2"	15	12	20
3-1/2" x 6-1/2"	16	8	4
9-1/2" x 9-1/2"	2		2
6-1/2" x 6-1/2"	1		1
3-1/2" x 9-1/2"	5		

5. Studying the diagram on page 40, piece each block, using the individual pieces where needed. Piece the border strips, alternating combinations. Study the diagram to see how to piece the four corners. Attach them to the side pieced borders.

6. Lay out blocks on the floor or on your bed and rearrange until you are satisfied. Join the blocks into rows with 15-1/2" lattice strips.

7. Join rows with 51-1/2" lattice strips.

8. Add outside lattice strips, sides first, then top and bottom.

9. Add the pieced border to the top and bottom of the quilt.

10. Sew the side plain border to the side pieced border (which includes the pieced corners). Sew this border unit to the quilt.

11. Finally, sew on the top and bottom plain borders.

Finishing

Due to the variety of patterns, I suggest Continuous Curve Quilting or hand quilting for this quilt. Ernest Haight's Machine Quilting Method would not be suitable.

Finish in the traditional way (see page 180) and machine quilt. Then finish the edge by making 3"-wide continuous binding, folded in half (see page 182).

For more information, consult Part Four: Machine Quilting.

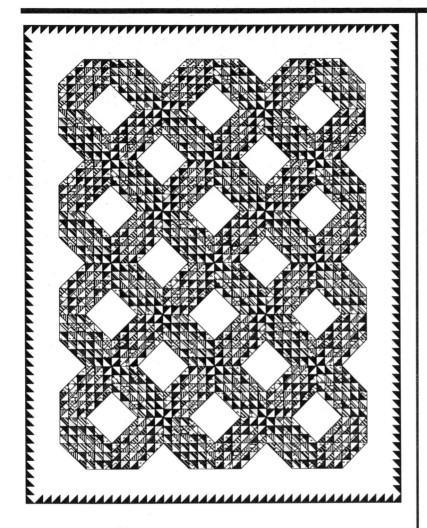

Half-Square Triangles: Ocean Waves

This quilt block is made from four sections of triangles surrounding a center square on point. At first glance the blocks may seem identical, but there are actually two different blocks. In studying the diagram on page 48, notice that the B blocks are offset vertically from the A blocks. This is called a half-drop grid (see page 188). Because of the different placement of lights and darks in the two blocks, the triangles or waves "move" in different directions. A secondary design of pinwheels will occur where the "waves" intersect at the top and bottom of blocks if you always use the same light and dark combinations in these positions.

King, 93" x 119"

Time—long time due to the small size of the triangles

Difficulty—less difficult than it looks, but the triangles are small

Seam allowance: 1/4"

Finished size of small square:
2-1/8"

Marking size of grid: 3"

Finished size of large square:
9-1/4"

Finished size of rectangle:
12-3/4" x 25-1/2"

Number of full blocks: 18

Width of plain border: 6"

Width of pieced border: 2-1/8"

Combinations needed:
1152 Half-Square Triangles of
light prints/dark prints,
196 Half-Square Triangles of dark
prints/background (for border)

Yardage

Quilt top:

Light prints: 1/2 yard each of 9 different light
prints (= 4-1/2 yards) or 3/8 yard each of 16
different light prints (=6 yards)—The smaller the
pieces of yardage, the greater the total amount of
yardage that must be used.

Dark prints: 1/2 yard each of 9 different dark prints
or 3/8 yard each of 16 different dark prints

7 yards of background fabric for triangles, plain
blocks, and borders

1 yard dark fabric for border triangles

Backing: 8 yards

Binding: 1 yard

Recommended batting: See page 179.

Making the Quilt Top

Pieces You Will Need for the Blocks

	Piece	Number of Pieces		
		Light Prints	Dark Prints	Background Fabric
1. Triangle Combinations Make Half-Square Triangle combinations following the general instructions. Mark at 3" intervals. Use 1/4" seam allowance.		← 1152 combinations → ← 196 combinations →		
2. Single Triangles Mark Half-Square Triangles following the general instructions. Mark at 3" intervals. Cut out after marking.	 	144		144
3. Cut out a 9" square template from cardboard. Place it on the wrong side of the fabric. Mark around it. Cut out at least 1/4" larger.	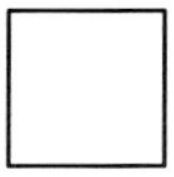			18
4. To make the template for the Half-Square Triangles, cut the square template in half diagonally.	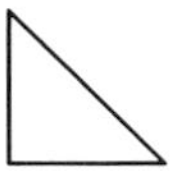			10
5. Cut the template in half again to make these last four triangles.	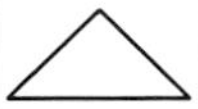			4

1. For the plain border, cut four 6-1/2"-wide strips from your length of background fabric, two approximately 108" long for the sides and two approximately 93" long for the ends. Cut to the proper length after your blocks are made.

2. You will need a total of 9 – 12 yards of light and dark prints for the blocks (see note above about yardage). Make 1152 Half-Square Triangle combinations following the general instructions on page 25. Mark the grid at 3" intervals. Make extras to allow for imperfections.

3. Cut lengths of 1 yard each of dark print and background fabric for the pieced border. Mark the grid at 3" intervals and make at least 196 Half-Square Triangle combinations. Set aside.

4. The tops of the triangles that surround each center square call for individual triangles to be pieced to combinations. Use the same method as shown on page 27 to mark a 3" grid on 1/2 yard each of dark and light prints, but don't mark the sewing lines—only the square grid with diagonal lines. Make all diagonal lines parallel, as shown on page 13. Cut out the square grid, then the diagonal lines, to make 144 each light and dark print triangles.

5. Sew the triangle combinations and single triangles together to make four kinds of triangle sections. Make 24 of each section. You will use 18 for the full A and B blocks and the remainder for partial B blocks.

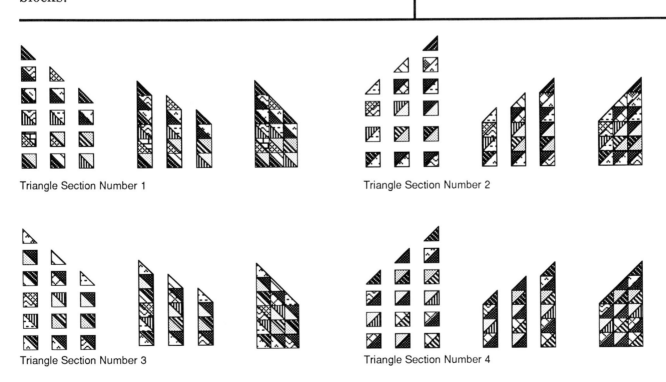

Triangle Section Number 1

Triangle Section Number 2

Triangle Section Number 3

Triangle Section Number 4

Chapter 3. **Half-Square Triangles**   **45**

Cut 18 background squares.

Cut 10 background triangles.

Cut 4 background triangles.

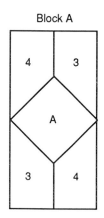
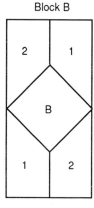

Two Different Rectangular Blocks

6. Now we must cut individual shapes for the center squares and to fill out the sides of the quilt top. We waited to cut out these background pieces until we could measure the slanted side of the triangle sections. While this side should measure approximately 9-3/4", yours may differ slightly. Adjust the size accordingly. We will make a template of the finished size of the center square, then cut the template up to make other templates.

Cut a 9-1/4" square template from plastic or cardboard. This is the *finished* size of the square. (Subtract 1/2" from whatever your measurement is if it differs from this.) Place the template on the wrong side of the fabric. Mark around it. This is the *sewing* line. Cut out at least 1/4" larger all around. Cut 18 squares from background fabric.

7. Now we'll make a template for the triangles in the partial blocks at the edge of the quilt top. Cut the square template from Step 6 in half diagonally. This is the *finished* size of the triangle marked X. Mark the straight of grain on the long side in pencil. Place the template on the wrong side of the fabric, matching grainlines. Mark around it. This is the *sewing* line. Cut out at least 1/4" larger all around. Cut 10 triangles from background fabric. Label them X. When these triangles are pieced into the quilt top, their outside edge will be on the straight of grain.

8. Cut the template in half again to make the last four triangles, to be pieced into the four corners of the quilt top. Erase the grainline from Step 7. Mark the grainline along one of the short sides. Place the template on the wrong side of the fabric, matching grainlines. Mark around it. This is the *sewing* line. Cut out at least 1/4" larger all around. Cut 4 triangles from background fabric. Label them Y. When these triangles are pieced into the quilt top, their outside edges will be on the straight of grain.

9. Sew the triangle sections and the squares of background fabric together to make the blocks.

Block A is made from Number 3 and Number 4 triangle sections around background squares. Make 12 blocks. Put them in a stack and label them.

Block B is made from Number 1 and Number 2 triangle sections around background squares. Make 6 blocks. Put them in a stack and label them.

10. There are also partial B blocks. These use the two sizes of triangles cut in Steps 7 and 8, rather than squares, combined with the remaining pieced triangle sections from Step 5. You will need to make the combinations shown at right.

11. Lay out the blocks and partial blocks on a large surface. It's easier to lay out the first vertical column of A blocks, then the half-dropped column of B blocks. When you have all the full blocks in position, lay out the partial blocks. Double-check your layout against the quilt on page 43. Are your waves in a logical way? If not, check to be sure you haven't switched blocks. Join the blocks vertically into columns. Then join the columns to make the quilt top.

12. Sew the plain border to the sides of the quilt top, then the top and bottom.

13. Piece the dark print/background Half-Square Triangle combinations into a line, with the dark half on the right side of each combination. Measure your quilt top to see how long each side border piece should be. Sew the pieced border to the sides. If you have mismeasured, adjust the plain border to fit the pieced squares. Sew pieced borders to the top and bottom.

Finishing

Baste in the traditional manner (see page 180). I suggest machine quilting with Continuous Curve Quilting, using a series of repeating vertical paths. This will cover most of the pieced areas of the quilt. The remaining isolated areas will need to be quilted individually. Bind the edge with bias binding cut 2" wide and folded in half.

For more information, consult Part Four: Machine Quilting.

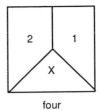

four

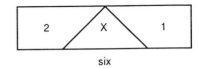

six

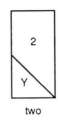 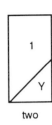

two   two

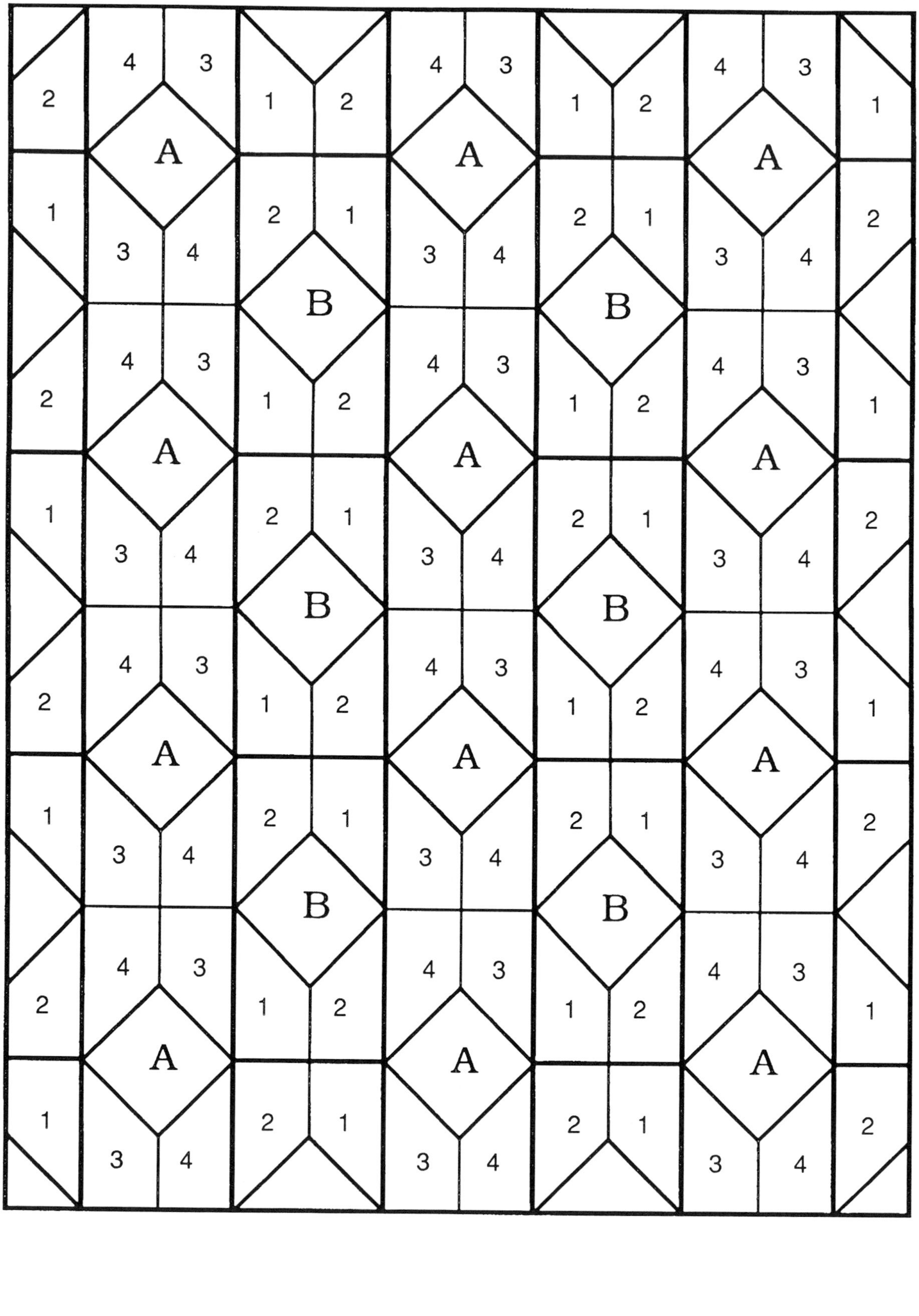
A
B
1
2
3
4

Now that you have grasped the principles of Crystal Piecing (mark, sew, cut) and experimented with Half-Square Triangles, you will find it easy to make Quarter-Square Triangles.

If you are not familiar with the term, imagine a square divided into quarters. The four resulting triangles are Quarter-Square Triangles. When they occur in pairs or sets of pairs, that is a signal to mass-produce or speed-piece them with the following method. While not as common as Half-Square Triangles in traditional patchwork, Quarter-Square Triangles nonetheless expand your options in Crystal Piecing.

Again you must understand the difference between the marking size and the finished size. When using 1/4" seams, there is a 1-1/4" difference between the marked size and the finished size. As with Half-Square Triangles, if you mark the grid in fractions, you will finish in whole inches. If you mark in whole numbers, you will finish in fractions. Decide which way to go based on what shapes and sizes you will be making.

While it is possible to mark with a straight edge and grid, many quilters find the required successive addition of fractions difficult. It is far easier to use the lines on a large plastic ruler. (See pages 16 – 17 for a more complete discussion.)

If you are unfamiliar with Quarter-Square Triangles, read through the instructions. Then practice on scraps of fabric before plunging in on the project you have in mind.

4.◆ Quarter-Square Triangles

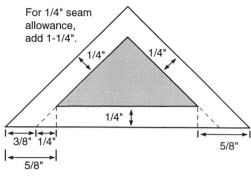

For 1/4" seam allowance, add 1-1/4".

1/4"   1/4"

1/4"

3/8" 1/4"   5/8"

5/8"

5/8" + 5/8" = 10/8" = 1-2/8" = 1-1/4"

Finished Size of Square	Marking Interval
2"	3-1/4"
2-3/4"	4"
4"	5-1/4"
5-3/4"	7"

Tip You can save yourself a lot of aggravation caused by mismarking if you premark the ruler with tape. Near each end, place small pieces of tape at the 4-1/4" line. An easily removable tape like Post-It Notes works well for a few triangles; use masking tape for marking many triangles.

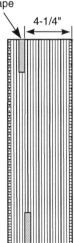

Tape

4-1/4"

Determining the Marking Size

For Half-Square Triangles, we allowed for the 1/4" seam allowance on the diagonal of the square. (See page 25.) Thus, we added 7/8" to the finished size of the square when using a 1/4" seam allowance.

For Quarter-Square Triangles, we have two diagonals. Therefore we must add 1-1/4" to the finished size.

1. Decide on the finished size of the squares.

2. Add on the Quarter-Square Triangle seam allowance.

Constructing the Triangles

1. For this demonstration, use light and dark fabrics the size of a fat half (18" x 21"). After determining what size you want the triangle to finish, add 1-1/4". In this example, you'll mark at 4-1/4" intervals and finish at 3". Of the two pieces of fabric you will be using, mark the wrong side of the lighter fabric.

2. Mark vertically and horizontally at 4-1/4" intervals. Mark diagonally in one direction. These will eventually be cutting lines.

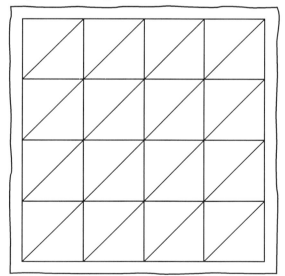

Barbara Johannah's Crystal Piecing

3. Working in the opposite diagonal direction, mark pairs of lines that are each 1/4" from the center of the square. These will be your sewing lines. If you are more comfortable marking the center diagonal line first, do so.

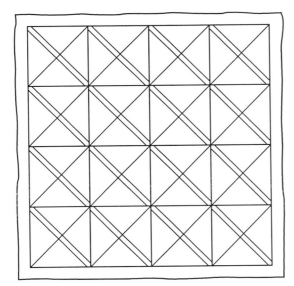

4. Place the piece you have just marked on your contrasting fabric, right sides together. Pin in each triangle as shown. This is to keep it from shifting while it is being sewn.

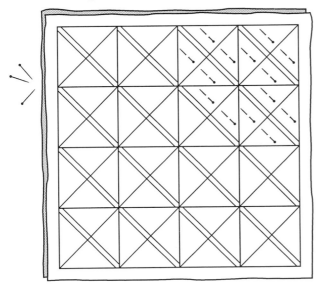

5. Sew on the paired diagonal lines that you have just drawn.

Tip I used to use a clear, plastic ruler to mark these sewing lines, aligning the line 1/4" from the edge through the centers of each square and drawing a line along the edge. Then I flipped the ruler for the second sewing line, double-checking to be sure they were each 1/4" from the center.

Now I use a Little Foot presser foot. It's exactly 1/4" from the needle to the edge. With it, I just mark the center cutting line. I don't need to mark the sewing lines.

Tip If you don't like sewing over the tips, you can raise the presser foot and draw the fabric away from the needle until you reach the next sewing place. Lower the presser bar lever and continue sewing. Beware: This can pucker the fabric. Try both ways and decide for yourself.

" I've often wished I could see inside old quilts to see their construction. One of the reasons this method of piecing [Quick Quiltmaking] is so great is that once the quilt is quilted, you can't tell what construction method was used.

It makes it difficult, though, to refute some of the "myths" of quiltmaking. Enough people have told me of a relative who had pieced this way to give me a general impression of both its existence and its isolation. A few worked in this way but it was not generally known.**"**

1980 letter from Barbara Johannah to Joyce Peaden

Tip If you wish to have all of the Quarter-Square Triangles pairs be identical, follow one of these diagrams for marking and sewing.

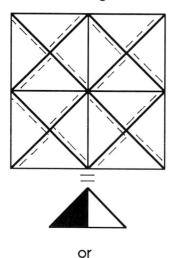

or

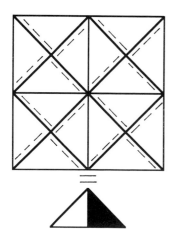

6. Cut on the vertical and horizontal lines to make squares. Cut each square in half between the stitching lines. Cut again on the single diagonal line that bisects each triangle.

7. Open triangles and press seam allowances towards the darker fabric if they would show through your lighter fabric. Trim the triangle pairs. When a 1/4" seam is taken around all three sides, they will finish 3-3/4" and the final square will finish 3". You now have a stack of pre-made Quarter-Square Triangle combinations. Note that the triangle combinations are of two types, with dark to either the left or the right.

Barbara Johannah's Crystal Piecing

Quarter-Square Triangles: Ohio Star

Even though you see the Ohio Stars in this quilt top, you don't piece individual blocks. Rather, you construct the central part of the quilt top in horizontal rows.

We are marking the triangles in whole inches and finishing in fractions.

King, 103" x 120"
Difficulty—average
Time—average

Seam allowance: 1/4"

Finished size of small white square: 5-3/4"

Marking size of grid: 7"

Size of large square: 11-1/2"

Number of Ohio Stars: 24

Width of borders: 17-1/4"

Quarter-Square Triangle combinations needed:

48 combinations of #1/#4

48 combinations of #4/#1 (reversed)

48 combinations of #1/#2

48 combinations of #2/#1 (reversed)

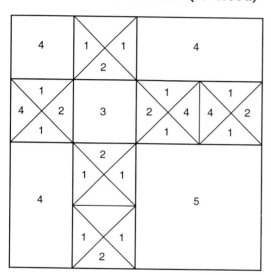

Yardage

Quilt top:

 Position #1   2-1/2 yards

 Position #2   1-1/4 yards

 Position #3   1 yard

 Position #4   7 yards

 Position #5   1-1/2 yards

Backing: 9 yards

Binding: 1-1/4 yards

Batting: See chart, page 179.

Making the Quilt Top

Pieces You Will Need

	Piece	Number of Pieces				
		Dark Solid #1	Large Print #2	Small Squares #3	Background Fabric #4	Large Squares #5
1. Quarter-Square Triangle Combinations Make the combinations following the general instructions on page 49. Mark the grid at 7". (If you mark the seam lines following the general instructions, you will automatically get half of them reversed.)		← 48 →				
		← 48 →				
		← 48 →				
		← 48 →				
2. Small Single Squares 6-1/4" x 6-1/4"				24		
					20	
3. Single Rectangles 6-1/4" x 12"					14	
4. Large Squares 12" x 12"						12

5. Lay out the central part of the quilt top on a large surface, following the diagram. You will be piecing 11 horizontal rows. Four of them are twice as big as the others and you must piece four sets of two Quarter-Square Triangle combinations together, one above the other, before you can piece the row.

6. Piece horizontally; then piece rows into the central portions.

1. Set aside fabric for the large border pieces. Cut to size after measuring the complete center of the top. Approximate sizes:

two 17-3/4" x 69-1/2"

two 17-3/4" x 86-3/4"

2. Make Quarter-Square Triangle combinations following the general instructions on page 49. Mark the grid at 7" intervals. If you mark the seam lines following the general instructions, you will automatically get half of the combinations reversed.

3. Now cut the individual pieces that will be combined with the Quarter-Square Triangles to make rows. Cut these individual pieces, enough for the central part of the quilt top and the four corner Ohio Stars:

24 small single squares (#3) 6-1/4" x 6-1/4"

20 small single squares (#4) 6-1/4" x 6-1/4"

14 rectangles (#4) 6-1/4" x 12"

12 large squares (#5) 12" x 12"

4. Lay out the central part of the quilt top on a large surface, following the diagram. You will be piecing 11 horizontal rows. Four of them are twice as high as the others and you must piece four sets of two Quarter-Square Triangle combinations together, one above the other, before you can piece the row.

5. Piece horizontally; then piece rows into the central portions.

6. Construct the four Ohio Stars in the corners as individual blocks.

7. Measure the central part of the quilt on the sides. Cut borders to fit. Piece the four Ohio Stars to top and bottom borders. Piece plain borders to sides of quilt. Piece remaining borders to top and bottom.

Finishing

Baste the quilt in the traditional way (see page 180). Use either Stitch-in-the-Ditch or Continuous Curve Quilting. Make two vertical and horizontal passes for each row or column of Ohio Stars. Then stitch diagonally in a large zigzag pattern along the dark Quarter-Square Triangles and flowered fabric, two passes per row. This leaves Positions #3 and #5 for isolated quilting. Bind the edges with a 3" continuous binding folded in half.

For more information, consult Part Four: Machine Quilting.

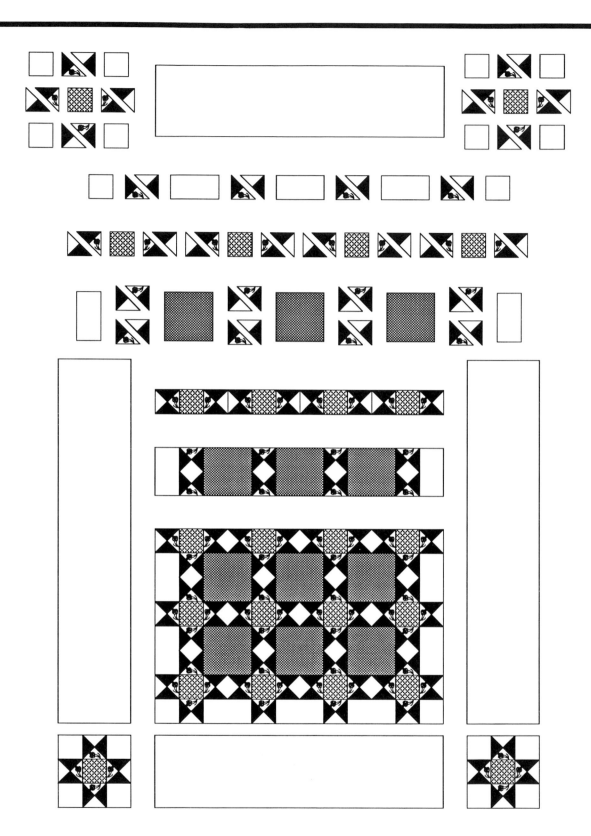

Starwheels

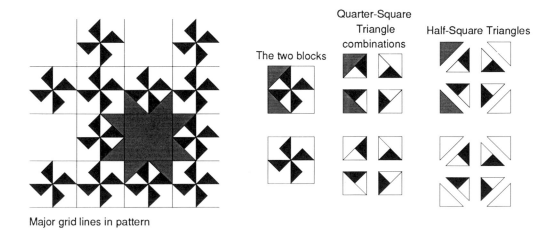

Major grid lines in pattern

The two blocks

Quarter-Square Triangle combinations

Half-Square Triangles

Chapter 4. **Quarter-Square Triangles** **57**

5.

Other Jewels

❝ All our knowledge has its origins in our perceptions. **❞**
Leonardo da Vinci

A mind shift has taken place in how quilters view the construction of quilts. Many people now automatically translate quilt patterns into speed-piecing techniques. But although people have made refinements of my approach, few new methods have appeared since my original book.

What you'll learn in this section is "new." It has evolved out of Crystal Piecing the Snowball pattern. This way of approaching piecing unlocks all sorts of possibilities. I call this material "new," but actually, I included the following method for Snowball in my first book, *Quick Quilting—Make A Quilt This Weekend,* in 1976, along with Strips and Strata and Half- and Quarter-Square Triangles, but no one picked up on it. I guess it was just too much to comprehend all at once. (That my publisher put my pitiful drawings in the book and put them out of order may have contributed.) I left Snowball out of the next book and it sank into oblivion, along with its potential.

Now is the time to show Snowball again and all of the wonderful possibilities that happen when you extend Crystal Piecing beyond Half- and Quarter-Square Triangles.

The construction sequence is the same as with Half- and Quarter-Square Triangles: mark, sew, and finally cut your fabric. There are differences, however. The marking is more complicated. I suggest you do it with several colors of pencils, one for each step, until this method is an old familiar friend. Also, when you cut, sometimes you cut through one layer and sometimes through two layers.

With some of the patterns, notably Snowball, you will have unused fabric. I hesitate to call this waste fabric, as it is all precisely cut to specific dimensions. I think of it as a resource for future projects.

That's it. That's all you need to learn to unlock the incredible possibilities of Crystal Piecing.

Wallhanging, 28" x 28"

Time—fast

Difficulty—easy once you understand the method

Yardage

Quilt top:

1 yard each of two fabrics (dark and light)

Backing: 1 yard

Recommended batting: See page 179.

Note: You will also need three colored pencils.

Jewels: Snowball

In the traditional Snowball quilt, two blocks with reverse coloring alternate to make the pattern. Using the Crystal-Piecing method, you mark one piece of fabric, sew it to the second, and finally cut the piece apart into finished blocks. Unlike Half- and Quarter-Square Triangles, you don't have further piecing to complete the block. With Snowball you end up with completed blocks.

Once you understand the method, the sewing is easy. Because of the large size of the pieces being marked, it would be easiest to do the marking with a straight edge on a grid, rather than using lines on a ruler.

There are better ways than using Crystal Piecing to make this particular block. It would be better to sew four small squares diagonally in the corners, trimming them to make triangles (you throw away the other half of the triangle). See page 62.

However, it's important to work something like this small wallhanging once, so you can understand the concept of Crystal Piecing. Snowball is a good pattern to start with. Then you can progress through the other approaches in this section more readily.

Notice that you will have precisely cut pieces leftover. Save them for future projects.

Seam allowance: 1/4"

Finished size of block: 4-1/2"

Marking size of grid: 5"

Number of blocks: 25

| Tip | Robbie Fanning prefers to cut one or two yards in half parallel to the selvage for easier marking and handling.

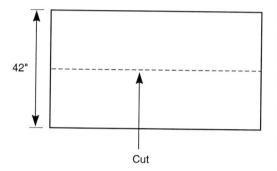

Cut

Making the Quilt Top

1. Cut out the border strips before making the blocks. Trim to fit after sewing them on the quilt top.

From the light fabric:

four strips 2" x approximately 28"

From the darker fabric:

four strips 3" x approximately 32"

The extra 1" width is to allow for a self-binding. Cut remaining pieces of fabric in half.

2. Note that half of the blocks are in the reverse coloration. Mark one half each of your remaining fabric in the following manner. With a colored pencil, mark the wrong side of the fabric vertically and horizontally into 5" squares. These will later be cutting lines. Mark enough for 13 light and 12 dark squares.

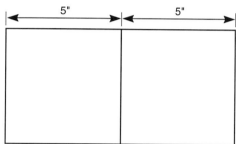

3. Using a second color of pencil, mark within the squares two vertical and two horizontal lines at the intervals shown.

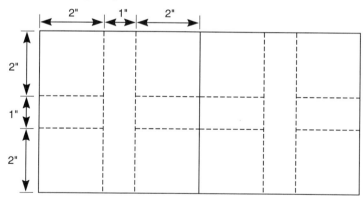

| **Barbara Johannah's Crystal Piecing**

4. With a third colored pencil, mark diagonally the corners of each 5" square, connecting the pairs of points A in each 2" square.

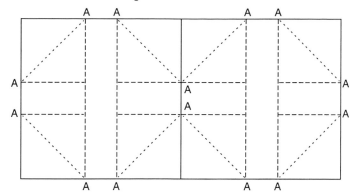

5. Place this marked piece of fabric right sides together on top of your contrasting fabric. Pin on both sides of the diagonal lines and at the edges of the central marked cross.

6. Sew through both layers of fabric on the diagonal lines you marked in Step 4.

7. Cut through both layers of fabric on the gridlines you drew in Step 2. This creates 5" squares.

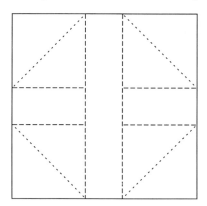

8. Cut the surplus fabric off the corners of each block, outside the diagonal lines you marked in Step 4.

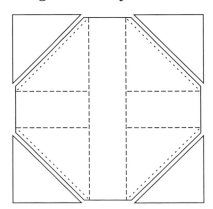

" I learned to strip-piece traditional blocks from my grandmother before I went to school (1931) and put that knowledge into use as a teenager. I was teaching a class in strip piecing in 1979 – 1980 when a friend, seeing my work, exclaimed, "Joyce, there is a new book out that is the same as what you are doing!"

It was an exhilarating experience to open Barbara's book and see this piecing which I had called "peasant work," because it is a practical way of putting quilts on beds. Barbara's book shone with clarity and organization.

I believe that my knowledge of the field put me in the best position to appreciate what she had done.

As for those two-triangle squares, I had never thought of putting two pieces of material together and sewing them in such a way as to produce two-triangle squares. I felt as though I had discovered the atom, as I read Barbara's work. I saw in my mind how the little squares would come out neat and clean. "

Joyce B. Peaden, inventor
Needletec Stencils
Prosser, WA

Another way of making Snowball is called Square in the Corner. (I would like to credit the inventor, but have not been able to find her or him. Perhaps you know whom to thank for this simple and clever idea.)

Use the chart on page 63 to find the size block and the size square you want. Cut slices; then cut squares off them.

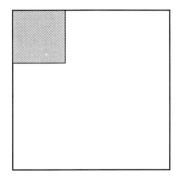

Sew an individual square in each corner.

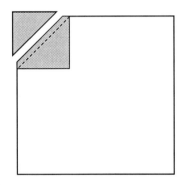

Trim corners.

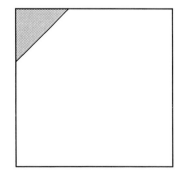

Press triangle out. Repeat for other corners.

9. Cutting through only the **top layer of fabric**, cut on the remaining lines that form a cross. Again, you will have precise pieces of fabric leftover. If you think it's easier to cut long strips rather than short rectangles, cut through the entire top layer of marked and sewn yardage (Step 9) before cutting along the gridlines to make 5" squares (Step 7).

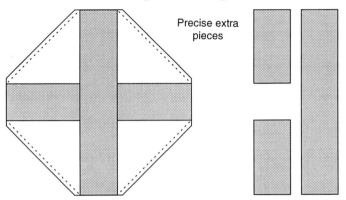

Precise extra pieces

10. Unfold the top triangles to reveal the finished Snowball block. Press seam allowances toward the dark fabric.

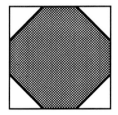

11. Repeat the entire procedure, but this time sew with the contrasting fabric on top.

12. Sew the light borders to the sides, then the top and bottom. Repeat with the dark border.

Finishing

Baste in the traditional manner (see page 180). While you could use Continuous Curve Quilting, the pathways would be difficult to find while sewing. Try Stitch-in-the-Ditch horizontally and vertically. For more information, consult Part Four: Machine Quilting.

Enough fabric has been allowed in the outer border for you to turn it to the back as a self-binding.

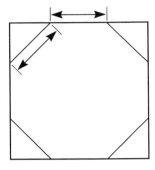

These two measurements finish at equal sizes or close to it.

For a true octagon appearance suitable for setting continuously

Finished size of block	Mark this size for block	Intervals to mark within block		
3-1/2"	4"	1-1/2"	1"	1-1/2"
5"	5-1/2"	2"	1-1/2"	2"
6"	6-1/2"	2-1/4"	2"	2-1/4"
8-1/2"	9"	3"	3"	3"
11-1/2"	12"	4"	4"	4"

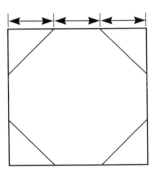

These three measurements finish at equal sizes.

For a nine-patch grid appearance, use this chart if combining with other nine-patch based blocks (such as the Twist.)

Finished size of block	Mark this size for block	Intervals to mark within block		
3"	3-1/2"	1-1/2"	1/2"	1-1/2"
4-1/2"	5"	2"	1"	2"
6"	6-1/2"	2-1/2"	1-1/2"	2-1/2"
7-1/2"	8"	3"	2"	3"
9"	9-1/2"	3-1/2"	2-1/2"	3-1/2"
10-1/2"	11"	4"	3"	4"
12"	12-1/2"	4-1/2"	3-1/2"	4-1/2"

Using some of the "waste" fabric

To use some of the triangular pieces left over after cutting, you could mark additional sewing lines 1/2" from the first diagonal lines marked. When you sew in Step 6 (page 61), also do these.

Cut out the squares. Then cut in between the parallel rows of stitching.

These tiny pieces become perfect Half-Square Triangles in a smaller size.

To save even more fabric, repeat the process with the border fabric.

Where will you use them? On the back, appliquéd in the centers of the Snowballs, on clothing, on gift cards—use your imagination!

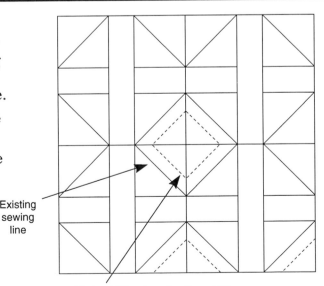

Existing sewing line

Mark additional sewing lines 1/2" over. Cut in between parallel rows of stitching to save even more fabric. Repeat the process with the border fabric.

Chapter 5. **Other Jewels** **63**

A-29

B-20

C-16

D-12

E-8

F-4

G-32

Snowball Variation

While Snowball is traditionally worked in two fabrics, the method lends itself to experimenting with many fabrics. In this variation of Snowball a different look has been achieved by having the fabrics change from dark to light as they move to the center. I'd make this with 8-1/2" blocks for a full-sized quilt.

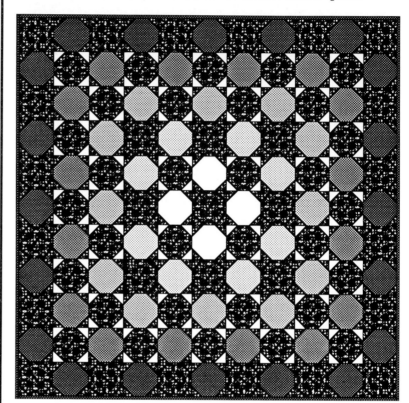

A	B	A	B	A	B	A	B	A	B	A
B	G	C	G	C	G	C	G	C	G	B
A	C	G	D	G	D	G	D	G	C	A
B	G	D	A	E	A	E	A	D	G	B
A	C	G	E	G	F	G	E	G	C	A
B	G	D	A	F	A	F	A	D	G	B
A	C	G	E	G	F	G	E	G	C	A
B	G	D	A	E	A	E	A	D	G	B
A	C	G	D	G	D	G	D	G	C	A
B	G	C	G	C	G	C	G	C	G	B
A	B	A	B	A	B	A	B	A	B	A

Quartz

This is simply Snowball cut horizontally and repieced.

What other patterns can you apply this approach to?

Assemble the block.

The complete block.

Mark

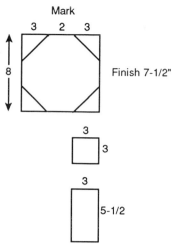

8

Finish 7-1/2"

See bottom chart on page 63.

Diamond Twist

Again, we're using partial blocks around the perimeter. Inside, the pattern breaks down into a Nine-Patch variation. Choose your measurements for Snowball from the bottom chart on page 63. One possible set of numbers is at left.

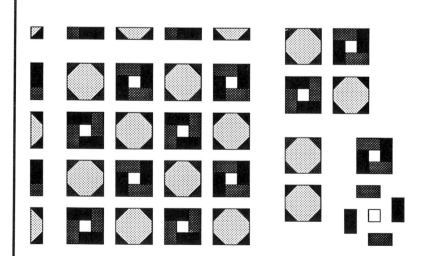

Fire Opal

This is the same idea as Snowball: marking, sewing, then cutting yardage—except here we mark and cut rectangles instead of squares.

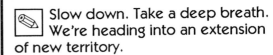

Slow down. Take a deep breath. We're heading into an extension of new territory.

You may not understand at first. That's OK. Persist.

While I am not giving full instructions, here are Crystal Piecing instructions.

1. Mark the top fabric in a rectangular grid. You must use a 1:2 ratio. Later you will cut on these lines.

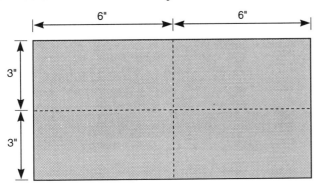

"Barbara Johannah's *Quick Quiltmaking Handbook* is still my favorite. Her clear and concise explanation of the fast-piecing techniques have led directly to three of my quilts, including one of my most successful, *King's X*.

I have studied the Half-Square Triangle design book with great interest. The infinite possibilities like personalized quilts with numerical or letter significance boggle the mind."

John Flynn, author
Braided Border Workbook
Billings, MT

Using some of the "waste" fabric

To use some of the triangular pieces left over after cutting, you could mark additional sewing lines 1/2" from the first diagonal lines marked. When you sew in Step 3, also do these.

Cut out the rectangles. Then cut in between the parallel rows of stitching.

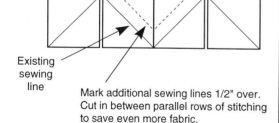

Existing sewing line

Mark additional sewing lines 1/2" over. Cut in between parallel rows of stitching to save even more fabric.

2. Use a second color of pencil to bisect the rectangles. Later these will be cutting lines through the **top layer only**.

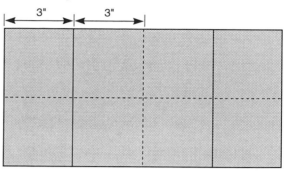

3. Use a third color of pencil to mark alternating diagonal lines through each square. Put this marked fabric right sides together with a contrasting piece of fabric. Sew along the diagonal lines.

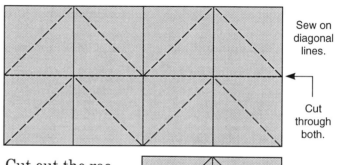

Sew on diagonal lines.

Cut through both.

4. Cut out the rectangles marked in Step 1.

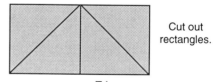

Cut out rectangles.

5. Trim off the corners outside the stitching through both layers. Cut on the center vertical line through the **top layer only**.

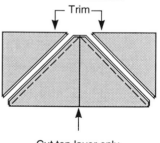

Trim

Cut top layer only.

6. Press the triangles to the outside.

7. When 1/4" seams are taken, here's how the unit will look:

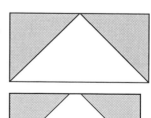

Press open

How the unit will look after a seam is taken.

Barbara Johannah's Crystal Piecing

Jewels: Garnet

Now that you understand the concept of Crystal Piecing squares and rectangles, let's apply it to a different situation: matching pieced yardage to plain yardage, then marking that for Crystal Piecing.

This first quilt uses a Checkerboard (see page 91) made with four fabrics instead of two.

One difference with this kind of piecing is that it's more fun if you design the quilt after you piece it. Crystal Piecing produces various combinations that are hard to predict in advance.

Surprise yourself!

Note: Once you cut, all of the edges are bias, so handle them carefully.

You will have extra fabric left over around the edges. How can you use it?

Wallhanging, 24-1/2" x 32-1/2"
Time—average
Difficulty—intermediate

Yardage

Quilt top:

    1/4 yard each of four small prints

    1 yard coordinating print

Backing: 1 yard

Binding: 1 yard

Recommended batting: See page 179.

Colored pencils

Seam allowance: 1/4"

Width of strips: 4-1/4"

Width of grid: 3-3/4"

Finished size of pillow: 3-1/4"

Finished size of block: 4"

Blocks needed: 48

Tip The final quilt design varies greatly, depending on how you repeat colors in the pieced yardage. Imagine piecing Sunshine and Shadow or Trip Around the World and then using it with Garnet.

Tip You can also mark in whole inches and have your blocks finish in fractions.

Making the Quilt Top

1. Cut 4-1/4"-wide crossgrain strips of the four small prints. You should have two strips of each print.

2. Seam the strips the long way in two sets of four. Press all seams open. Make sure the same color order is used in each set. Seam the sets together.

3. Cut across the strips every 4-1/4". Flip every other row. Now seam the rows together. Press seams open. You now have a small checkerboard.

4. Mark a square grid on the wrong side of the pieced checkerboard, connecting the *centers* of each pieced square to each other.

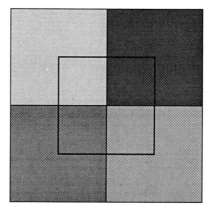

5. Right sides together, match the checkerboard to the coordinating print, with the pieced yardage on top. Stitch 1/4" inside the outside marked perimeter. Stitch 1/4" on either side of the inner grid.

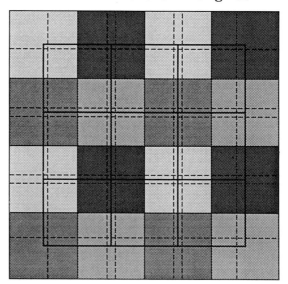

6. With a different colored pencil, mark an X through the center of each square marked and stitched. Since stitching may have distorted the cloth slightly, make sure the X crosses the intersection of the original checkerboard. If it is off, mark separately from the intersection out to the corner of each square. You may have to use different colors or kinds of marking devices, depending on the colors of your checkerboard.

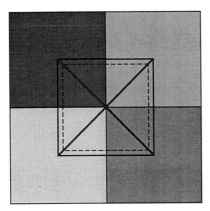

7. Cut out the squares marked in Step 4. I call these pillows.

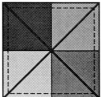

8. You will cut through the **top layer only** in this step. Pinch the center of the pillow, so you are holding only one layer. Insert scissors tips and cut along the X marked in Step 6.

9. Fold out the triangles and trim off tiny edges. Press the triangles carefully—these are all bias edges. You will have to make small clips through the stitching to get the triangles pressed properly. You have just Crystal Pieced 4-1/2" blocks like Snowball, but the combinations have Quarter-Square Triangles in the corners.

Tip When you cut out the pillows, you will have leftovers at the sides. If you cut through both layers of marked pencil lines, you will have Quarter-Square Triangles in pairs with Half-Square Triangles.

Tip You could press 4" squares of freezer paper to the back of the blocks, to keep them from stretching. This is an idea adapted from *Precision-Pieced Quilts Using the Foundation Method* by Jane Hall and Dixie Haywood.

✎ The first reaction of everyone is "But you will cut off the corners when you take 1/4" seams!"

My response is "So what?" This is what I mean when I say that quilt design may change when people grasp Crystal Piecing. Where is it decreed that corners must be squared?

10. Lay out your jewel combinations. Notice that 12 have one color on one side of the Quarter-Square Triangles and 12 have the same color on the other side. Sixteen combinations have two of the four colors; eight have the other two colors. Play with arranging these and the remaining combinations until you are pleased. Pin them to a piece of fabric until you can piece them.

11. You have lots of edges to match and all are bias. If you are a perfectionist, start in the center of each combination and stitch to the edge. Then flip the combination over and stitch from the center to the other edge. This helps prevent stretching.

Finishing

Baste well to prevent the quilt from stretching. Use Continuous Curve Quilting in the center areas. See Part Four: Machine Quilting for more information.

Cut 3"-wide continuous binding. Fold it in half and apply.

✎ Changing proportions of the pieced squares will change the look of the truncated tip. The larger the square, the less pronounced the cutting-off appears.

This is true of other Jewel shapes, too, like Emerald (see page 73).

Emerald

This is no different than Garnet, the previous design, except that you are marking rectangles.

If you'd like to try a simpler version, use two lengths of plain yardage, not one of pieced and one of yardage.

While I am not giving full instructions for the quilt, here are Crystal Piecing instructions.

1. Make a pieced top layer. Rectangles in a 1:2 ratio will be the easiest to work with, but other ratios are possible. Work as large a piece of fabric as feasible to make a more economical use of fabric and your time.

2. Mark vertically and horizontally to make a rectangle midway.

3. Use a second color of pencil to mark cutting lines. Because you made rectangles in a 1:2 ratio, you can use a ruler to mark diagonal lines; line up the corners of adjacent squares.

✏️ This is only a suggestion of how to cut. See Part Six: Barbara's Notebook for more ideas.

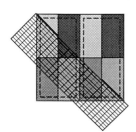
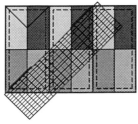

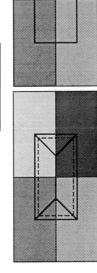

❝For the things we have to learn before we can do them, we learn by doing them.❞

Aristotle

4. Layer yardage right sides together with the pieced rectangles on top. Sew 1/4" inside the outside perimeter. Sew 1/4" on either side of the inner grid.

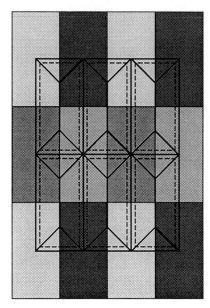

5. Cut out the rectangle pillows.

6. You will cut through the **top layer only** in this step. Pinch the center of the pillow, so you are holding only one layer. Insert scissors tips and cut along the lines marked in Step 3.

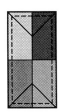

7. Fold out the shapes and trim off tiny edges. Press the shapes carefully where they have bias edges. You will have to make small clips through the stitching to get the shapes pressed properly.

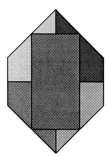

8. While you could try to piece this awkward shape (see color pages for a clever camouflage), it is much easier to assemble blocks if you square off the shape by adding triangles. You have two choices of where to add, one giving you a square and one, a rectangle.

The shape looks different when you take 1/4" seams. Here's how Shape A looks in various settings.

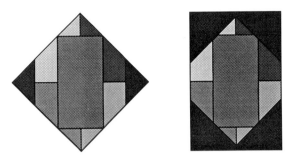

Before seam allowances

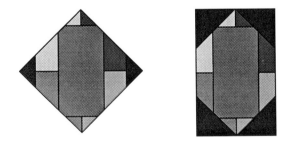

After seam allowances

Emerald Settings

Emerald is a block. Treat it like any other block. Then you will combine what you know about simple setting arrangements with a new kind of block.

Use the same approach with other jewels in this chapter. First do simple sets with one specific jewel. Experiment with color changes, as in the Snowball variation on page 64.

I hope quilters will combine different jewels, change sizes, free them from the grid, and try other processes which explore the potential of the new blocks.

Jewels: Sapphire

This Jewel pairs Half-Square Tri-angles with strip piecing. It's easy to work but looks complex—my favorite kind of quilt.

Wallhanging, 29" x 29"
Time—average
Difficulty—easy

Yardage

Quilt top:
  1/2 yard light fabric
  1/2 yard medium fabric
  1/2 yard dark fabric
Backing: 1 yard
Recommended batting: See page 179.

Making the Quilt Top

1. Cut all strips parallel to the lengthwise grain. Cut one strip from light fabric 3-3/4" wide. Cut the remainder of the fabric into 2-1/2"-wide strips. Cut the dark fabric into 2-1/2"-wide strips.

2. To make the four corner blocks, sew a dark/light/dark strata, using the wider light strip (3-3/4").

3. Slice across every 3-3/4", making four combinations.

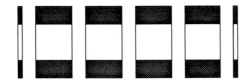

4. To finish the corner blocks, sew dark strips on each side of each strata. It's faster to sew two at a time to a dark strip, then cut them apart and trim. (If you don't understand the concept, refer to Log Cabin on page 105. These are constructed like Courthouse Steps.)

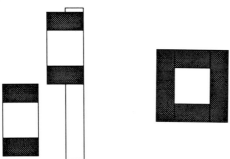

5. Now strip-piece light and dark strips together into strata.

6. On the wrong side, mark strata every 4-1/2" into squares. Mark diagonally, once in each square. Half are marked in one direction and half in another.

Seam allowance: 1/4"

Finished size of Half-Square Triangle: 3-3/4"

Marking size for grid: 4-1/2"

Width of strips for strata: 2-1/2"

Combinations needed: 48 plus four corner blocks

7. Place marked strata right sides together on medium fabric, strata side up. Don't leave any space between strata. They should touch each other. Pin profusely.

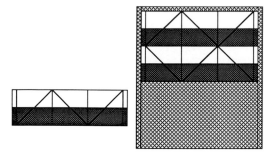

8. Sew 1/4" from each side of each diagonal line.

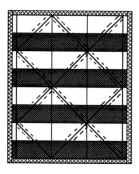

9. Cut horizontally between strata to make rows. Cut through both layers on the lines marked in Step 6 to make squares. Cut on the center diagonal line between stitching.

10. Press open into Half-Square Triangles in four combinations.

11. Assemble the quilt as shown.

Finishing

Use the Envelope Method (page 179) to finish and Stitch-in-the-Ditch of major design areas. See Part Four: Machine Quilting for more information.

Tip Linda Fry Kenzle, author of *Embellishments* (Chilton, 1993) plans to try this technique on crazy-quilted yardage matched with black velvet.

She suggests that any of the Jewel Crystal Piecing techniques would be a good way to rescue a partially pieced top that you've lost interest in.

Ruby

This idea is similar to Sapphire, but it uses four fabrics: a light color is strip-pieced to both dark and mid-gray fabric. These are then Crystal-Pieced to another fabric in Half-Square Triangles. You won't use all the shapes in this quilt; you'll have extras leftover for another one.

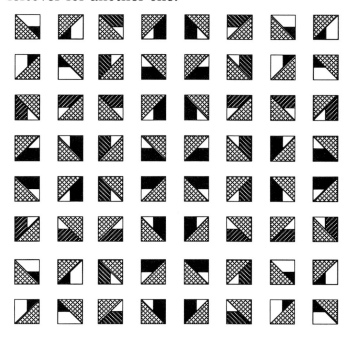

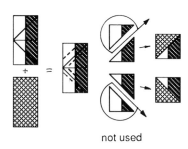

not used

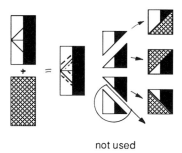

not used

Part Three:

Review of Strips and Strata

This section is organized by shapes and the quilts made from them: squares, rectangles, 45° angles, and equilateral triangles (be sure to read this section even if you are an experienced quilter—it has new ideas).

This section covers only piecing the tops, with suggestions for machine quilting. Finishing information is in Part Four: Machine Quilting.

6.

Strips and Strata: Mark/Cut/Sew

When my first book appeared in 1976, piecing quilts by the Strips and Strata method was rare. These methods are fairly common now, so I am reluctant to even include them.

But I've decided to include them as a reference section for three reasons.

1. New quiltmakers need information on piecing even the most elementary quilts, like Checkerboard. I want my son to be able to look here if he makes quilts.

2. Teachers covering the entire range of Quick Quiltmaking need a central reference for both kinds, Crystal Piecing and Strips and Strata. In addition, the Possibilities sections—new layouts and ideas for traditional patterns—can make even a beginner's quilt like Rail Fence exciting.

3. When you begin to analyze blocks for Quick Quiltmaking methods (see Chapter 14), you may need to refresh your memory on various techniques for Strips and Strata piecing.

Introduction to Strips and Strata

In the traditional way of piecing, you use a template to mark individual pieces, in preparation for cutting. This is slow. With quick-piecing methods, you use a plastic ruler, rotary cutter, and mat to measure and cut strips or a straight edge and a grid to mark strips for cutting. These long strips are subsequently sewn together into light/dark strata. (Strata are two or more strips of fabric sewed together along their long sides.) The strata are then marked and cut crosswise, resulting in rows of pre-sewn squares, rectangles, diamonds, or other shapes. These are called combinations. These shapes are combined further into a quilt block or entire quilt top.

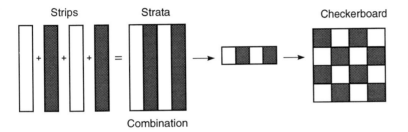

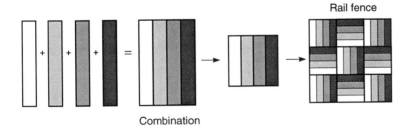

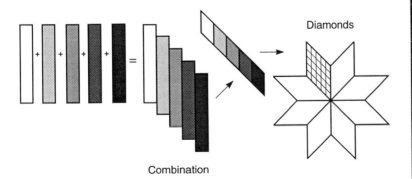

Nine-Patch

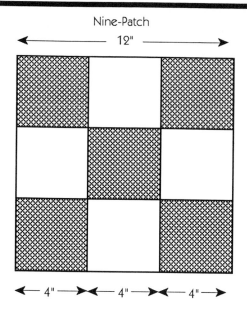

12"

← 4" →←← 4" →←← 4" →

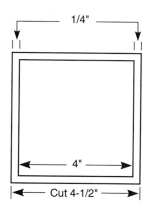

1/4"

4"

Cut 4-1/2"

Marking and Cutting Strips

To begin, you need to measure the finished width of your basic shape—square, rectangle, etc. Then decide on a seam allowance. If you choose a 1/4" seam allowance, for example, you must add 1/2" to the finished width to determine the cutting size for the strips.

Cut Size	Finished Size
4"	3-1/2"
3-1/2"	3"
4-1/2"	4"

To better help you understand the basics, I will use a 12" Nine-Patch block as an example in explaining Strips and Strata. (A Nine-Patch is nine 4" squares sewn together in three rows, three squares each.)

If the Nine-Patch block will be 12" when finished, then each of the finished pieces will be 4" square. Add 1/4" to all sides of one square for the seam allowance. This makes the marking and cutting interval 4-1/2".

Once you have determined your marking size, you are ready to begin. Choose between the following two methods of making strips. (See page 16 for a discussion of these tools.) For either, you need one yard each of light- and dark-colored fabric.

Method A:
Making strips with a plastic ruler, rotary cutter, and cutting mat

1. Fold a one-yard piece of fabric in half, selvages even, and in half again. The selvages must line up, but the short ends may not. It is now four layers thick.

2. Before cutting 4-1/2" strips, you must square one end. Be absolutely accurate when doing this next step. Trim 1/2" – 1" off one end so that it is at a perfect right angle to the folded edge. Place the plastic see-through ruler crosswise on the folded fabric. Align one of the ruler's crosswise gridlines on the fold.

Holding the rotary cutter blade in a vertical position, cut along the edge of the ruler. Cut slowly and firmly, rolling away from your body. Don't saw.

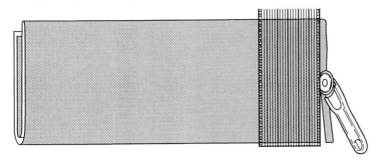

3. Now you can cut strips. Turn the folded fabric around. Using the 4-1/2" line on the ruler as a guide, cut off one strip.

4. Open up the strip. Is it perfectly straight? If it looks like a hockey stick, bent at the fold, the first trim cut was not measured correctly. Fold and cut again.

5. If it is straight, continue cutting every 4-1/2". Cut all the fabric into strips.

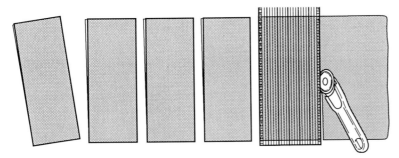

Method B:
Making strips with a grid, straight edge, pencil, and scissors

This method takes longer but is absolutely accurate. See page 16 for a longer discussion of these tools.

1. Place a piece of the lighter-colored fabric measuring 35" x 45" or less wrong side up on your grid. Line up the straight of the grain of the fabric with the lines marked on the grid.

2. Place the straight edge over the line on the grid nearest the edge of the fabric. Make sure your straight edge extends over the fabric at the top and bottom at least an inch. Use a sharp pencil. Hold the pencil at an angle with its tip as close to the straight edge as possible. Mark at 4-1/2" in one direction only.

Tip The longer the line you superimpose on the fabric edge, the easier it will be to get a true right angle. A long plastic ruler (e.g., 24" long) or a cutting mat printed with a grid are two ways of getting that long line.

I'm working with the yardage flat, not folded, because I have a huge drafting table. You may want to fold the fabric in half.

You can also use a rotary cutter with the ruler and dispense with the pencil marking.

If you have sharp scissors such as Ginghers, try marking only one piece of fabric. Layer up to eight pieces total, with the marked piece on top. Layer in light/dark pairs, right sides together. Carefully cut through all layers while the fabric is still on the board. Now peel off the top two. Right sides together, the edges are even and ready to sew. If you don't have sharp scissors, the layers may shift, causing inaccurate strips.

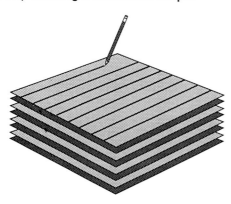

Beckie Olson, author of *Quilts by the Slice* (Chilton, 1992), prefers to cut strips on the lengthwise grain, which is more stable than the crosswise grain.

Don't sketch back and forth with the pencil. The first line acts as a baseline for the following marks.

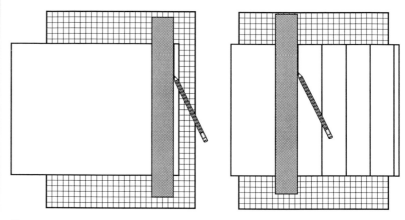

3. Following the lines you have drawn, cut the fabric into strips. The first strip is not used. Mark and cut your other fabric into strips as well.

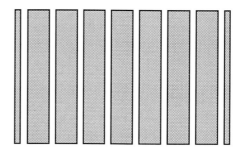

Alternate methods of marking and cutting your fabric

If you wish to mark a long length of your fabric, fold one end of the fabric. Mark as much as you can. Carefully unfold the unmarked end. Extend the lines using the previously marked lines as a guide. Measure crosswise occasionally to make sure you are maintaining the proper spacing.

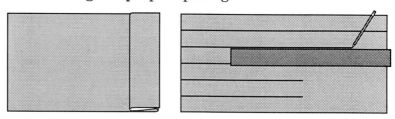

If you need very long pieces, such as for borders, you can press-mark a line. Fold your fabric parallel to the selvage at the width you need, press, and use the pressed line as a guideline for cutting.

Sewing Strips Into Strata

Arrange the strips in groups of three. Two-thirds of your strips will be sewn together in this order: dark strip, light strip, dark strip.

Barbara Johannah's Crystal Piecing

The rest of the strips will be sewn together in the reverse order: light strip, dark strip, light strip.

For example, from one yard of fabric you can cut approximately seven strips each of light and dark fabric. Two-thirds of 14 strips equals nine. Therefore, sew nine strata of dark/light/dark and five strata of light/dark/light.

Use a 1/4" seam allowance. (See page 15 for hints on accuracy in sewing.) Press the seam allowances away from the light fabrics. (See page 19 for a discussion of pressing.)

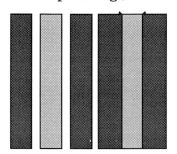

Making Combinations Into Blocks

Cut off the selvages. Mark strata crosswise at 4-1/2" intervals. Cut the strips crosswise on the line you have just drawn.

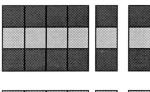

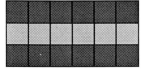

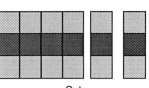

Mark   Cut

Sew three combinations together to complete the block. The middle combination is light/dark/light. Use a 1/4" seam allowance. Press all seams to one side.

Now combine the Nine-Patch blocks with plain blocks cut 12-1/2" square to make a quilt top.

Strata

2/3rds sewn this way

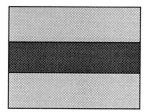

1/3rd sewn this way

Some people combine marking and cutting by using a rotary cutter and a plastic ruler.

Tip Blanche Young cuts with the seams up, so the strata don't shift under the ruler.

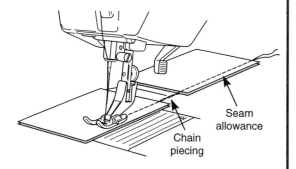

Seam allowance

Chain piecing

To cut 12-1/2" squares, either mark the fabric in both directions, then cut out:

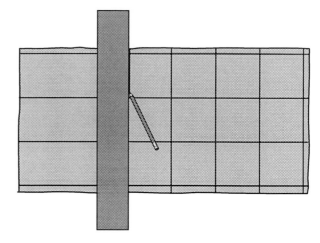

Or use a rotary cutter with a plastic ruler to cut 12-1/2" strips. Then cut across the strips to make 12-1/2" squares.

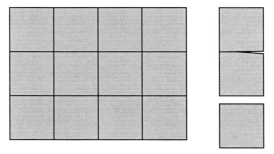

This is how most quilt tops are made from quick-cut, quick-pieced squares, rectangles, diamonds, etc. Any variations in this method are explained in the following sections. Once you have started, you will find that the actual process is incredibly fast.

Pointers on getting your intersections to meet

1. Seams pressed to one side

If you've pressed all seam allowances toward the dark side, when you sew combinations together, the seam allowances of one combination should lie one way and the seam allowances of the other combination the other way.

This creates "stair steps," which work to your advantage as they fit together. Have the seam allowance on top pointing toward the needle.

Pin the combinations at each intersection. Poke a pin straight through the intersections of the two combinations 1/4" from the edge. Now pin the two combinations together before and after the intersection, pinning 1/4" from the edge where the crosswise seam will run.

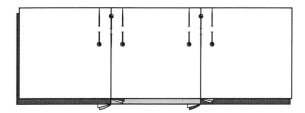

What if one square of the combination is a little too big for its matching square? It can be eased in.

Secure with pins or by sewing only in the intersections. Then sew in between, holding the fabric taut in front of and behind the needle. If your sewing machine grabs the bottom fabric and pushes away the top, be sure to have the longer piece on the bottom. The feed dogs will help ease it in.

Actually, I rarely pin to sew seams. I align the first intersection by eye and sew a 1/2" length seam only through it. I repeat this with each intersection. When finished with the row, I open it up and look at it. If any are off, I only have a 1/2" seam to rip out. I redo any that are off. When they're all accurate, I do the long seam, sewing over the previous sewing.

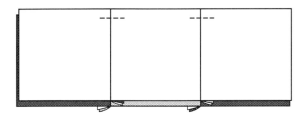

2. Seams pressed open

I'm a recent convert to pressing open seams. Press seams to one side first. Then open the seam allowances with your fingers as you press.

It's easier to match cross seams with opened seams but open seams are not suitable if you're going to machine quilt using Stitch-in-the-Ditch.

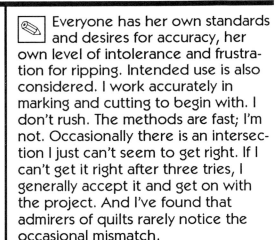

Everyone has her own standards and desires for accuracy, her own level of intolerance and frustration for ripping. Intended use is also considered. I work accurately in marking and cutting to begin with. I don't rush. The methods are fast; I'm not. Occasionally there is an intersection I just can't seem to get right. If I can't get it right after three tries, I generally accept it and get on with the project. And I've found that admirers of quilts rarely notice the occasional mismatch.

Finished is better than perfect.

I've yet to see the piece of work, which after being finished, could not be improved. Even in shows of the work of experts, one can find, if not a flaw, at least an aspect that might have been done better or differently. The maker herself often will say so. And among my quilting buddies, we can always find a better way.

There is a sure way to avoid making any mistakes: Don't do anything at all. Those who have never tackled a difficult piecing pattern or a complicated appliqué or a new quilting technique won't make any mistakes, but the rest of us who forge ahead have the joy of creativity, even with the peril of error.

Shirley Gould in Jan/Feb 1992
Quilter's Newsletter Magazine

7.

Squares

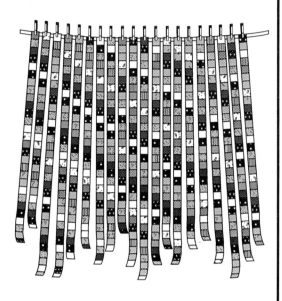

My First Quick-Pieced Quilt

After the fireworks explosion in my head, I was eager to try strip piecing. Gathering together the few suitable fabrics we had on hand, I searched out more. (This was the height of the polyester era and cotton fabrics were difficult to find.) After accumulating a satisfactory variety of fabrics, I thought I was ready.

Then I realized I didn't have any idea how I would make my accurate strips. What tools could I use? A trip to the fabric store yielded a cardboard cutting board. With the addition of a yardstick and a pencil, I was ready. I marked and cut strips and kept them in separate piles.

At the sewing machine, I placed as many of the stacks around me as I could. I sewed them together into strata, filling in with extras when the strips were short. Then I cut crosswise. It was exhilarating—so many perfect squares before me. I knew then I'd never finish the template-cut Irish Chain top I'd started earlier, its hundreds of little squares already cut out.

With the combinations cut, I placed them in tidy stacks all around the sewing machine. I had chosen Sunshine & Shadow, a simple pattern (see page 97). The pattern is staggered one square in each row. It sounded easy. Twenty rows across in my planned quilt meant twenty stacks to keep in order. Filled with confidence and the joy of this wonderful way of working, I sewed and cut over and over, always keeping my growing rows in orderly stacks, or so I thought.

With the rows almost complete, I began to realize that something was not going right. My rows, while all different, should have been all the same length as I worked. But some were very short and some were very long. I had made an error somewhere and now the error was compounding. I pinned them to the clothesline to take a look. What a mess! It was just as I feared. They were all different lengths and some were out of order. It was monstrously difficult to correct the problem, taking longer to rip and rearrange than it had to mark, cut, and sew in the first place—but no matter. I knew that from now on, this was the way to make quilts.

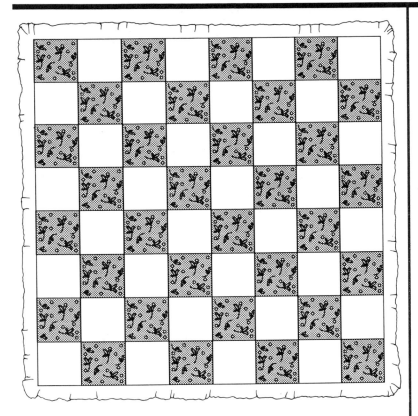

Squares: Checkerboard

This super-quick little baby quilt is ideal as a gift for a new-born. The eyelet fabric and lace ruffle make this simple checkerboard design special. We're using 1/2" seam allowances because of the eyelet. If you use regular fabric rather than eyelet, use 1/4" seams. The quilt will then finish 36" x 36".

Baby Quilt, 32" x 32"
Time—very fast
Difficulty—super simple

Yardage

Quilt top:
   5/8 yard eyelet
   5/8 yard print fabric
   4-1/4 yards pre-gathered lace, 3" – 4" wide
Lining for eyelet: 1 yard
Backing: 1 yard
Recommended batting: See page 179.

Seam allowance: 1/2"

Finished size of squares: 4"

Width of strips: 5"

Pieces needed: 32 print squares, 32 eyelet squares

Making the Quilt Top

1. Refer to the general instructions for working with Strips and Strata on page 82. Cut both the eyelet and the print fabric into four 5"-wide strips. Alternate light and dark strips.

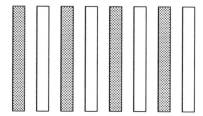

2. Sew the eight strips together.

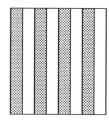

3. Press seam allowances to one side.

4. Cut crosswise every 5" into eight strips.

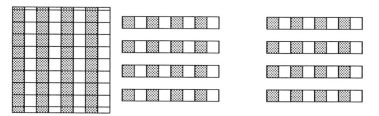

5. To make the checkerboard, turn every other row upside down. Sew the rows together to complete the top.

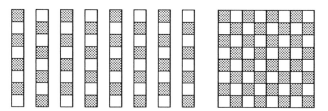

Barbara Johannah's Crystal Piecing

Finishing

Pin the pre-gathered lace to the right side of the top, the finished edge facing in. Be sure to allow extra lace at the corners. Finish the raw short ends of the lace. Since the eyelet has holes in it, you must line the quilt top with fabric. Baste 1/4" around all edges.

Then use the Envelope Method on page 179. See page 170 for how to use Continuous Curve Quilting on this quilt.

For more information, read Part Four: Machine Quilting.

" Trace, cut, and sew all those little pieces? Not for me—until I read Barbara Johannah's book in 1980. It "gave" me the freedom to create units of color and design suitable not just for quilts but for clothing and wall hangings. Teaching the technique has allowed me to share in the excitement of my students in exposing them to a revolutionary way of creating, combined with speed, accuracy, and quality. **"**

Judi Cull, co-author
Know Your New Home Sewing Machine
Sacramento, CA

Squares: Trip Around the World

Design Choices

Trip Around the World and its variations are the rainbows of quilts. Rather than contrasting light and dark, like Checkerboard, the colors often gradually blend into each other.

You could vary one color from light to dark, such as:

light blue
medium light blue
medium blue
dark blue

You could follow all or part of the rainbow:

yellow
yellow-orange
orange
orange-red
red

You could blend two colors in different ways:

light green	or	light green
medium green		medium green
dark green		dark green
light blue		dark blue
medium blue		medium blue
dark blue		light blue

Queen, 93" x 93"
Time—very fast
Difficulty—easy

Yardage

Quilt top:

1-1/2 yards each of 7 fabrics
(see discussion of color on the left)

Backing: 6 yards

Binding: 1 yard

Recommended batting: See page 179.

Making the Quilt Top

1. Refer to the general instructions on working with strips on page 82. Make the lengthwise strips 3-1/2" wide. (3" finished plus a 1/4" seam on each side.) You will cut about 12 strips from each color.

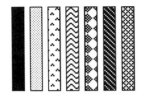

2. Sew the strips together in groups of seven along their long sides, using 1/4" seams.

3. Press seam allowances to one side.

4. Mark on the wrong side of the strata every 3-1/2". Cut into combinations on the lines marked. You will cut approximately 14 combinations from each strata.

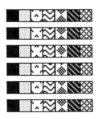

5. Trip Around the World is constructed in four sections. We will start with the upper left section of the quilt.

Notice that some of the rows need only part of a combination at the top and part at the bottom. For example, the first row has two whole combinations and one partial combination. Rip out the seam separating the combination into the two parts. The unneeded portion of a combination of one top is the needed portion of another row. They do not go to waste! Working on a large table or the floor, arrange the combinations following the diagram. The second row is pulled up or staggered one square. The third

Seam allowance: 1/4"

Finished size of squares: 3"

Width of strips: 3-1/2"

Pieces needed: 961 squares (set 31 squares x 31 squares)

row is staggered two squares. The fourth row is staggered three squares. The eighth row is back in the starting position. Sew the combinations together into rows.

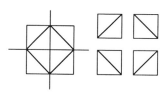

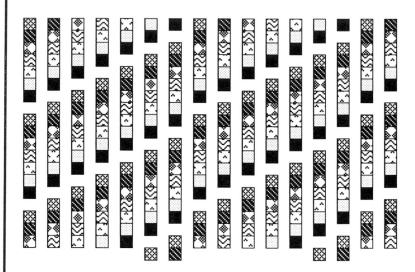

6. Sew the rows together.

7. Repeat with the other three sections. The heavy lines on the quilt on page 94 show where the quilt is to be divided into sections.

8. Join the four sections to complete the quilt top.

Finishing

Finish in the traditional way (see page 180). Bind the edge with continuous binding cut 3" wide and folded in half (see page 182).

Many choices are suitable for machine quilting this pattern. Of the machine quilting methods discussed in Part Four: Machine Quilting, Ernest Haight's method would be the easiest. If you choose to use Continuous Curve Quilting, you could quilt diagonally following the pattern or vertically and horizontally. The latter would be easier.

Anyone who stops learning is old, whether at 20 or 80. Anyone who keeps learning stays young. The greatest thing in life is to keep your mind young.

By rearranging the sequence of squares, all three of the following quilt patterns can be made in the same manner as Trip Around the World. Photocopy the diagrams. Then try coloring in the diagrams to see what color combinations you like.

Sunshine and Shadow

Worked in rows, rather than sections. This quilt works just as well in a rectangular size.

Zig Zag

Worked in rows. This quilt works just as well in a rectangular size.

Center of the World

Made in sections.

Here I played with the basic Trip Around the World on my computer. I selected an area of the pattern and offset it, filling in the empty space with other sequences of squares.

In the second design, I started by offsetting parts, as in the previous quilt. Then I repeated half of the pattern on either side.

This is lots of fun and the results are pure serendipity. I do these on the computer in what seems like minutes (the clock says it takes longer).

Drawing one Trip Around the World and making many photocopies is just as fast as the computer, I think. Cut the copies up, reposition, overlap, create space, and fill in to create new Trip Around the World variations. See Chapter 13 for more ideas on designing your own quilts.

If you wish to design your own all-over squares quilt, consider these variables:

1. The number of squares in your sequence or repeat.

2. The finished size of your square: 3" – 4" is suggested for most quilt makers, 1" – 2" for those who want a challenge, 5" for those with minimal sewing skills or who are in a hurry.

The smaller the square and the longer the repeat, the greater the richness and subtlety of the finished quilt.

Don't dismiss Rectangles as ordinary. See the Possibilities on page 104 and think of applying the same principles of arrangement to other blocks.

See also the rectangular shapes in Crystal Piecing (page 73).

Trip by Rail

8. ◆

Rectangles

Rectangles: Rail Fence

Rail Fence is but one of many patterns which can be made with this versatile, simple block. The fabrics in the Rail Fence progress from dark to light. Other patterns may use the same progression or may have the dark on the inside or on both outsides. When your blocks are completed, try the setting arrangements given here and then design your own before making a final decision. Variations are shown on page 104.

Lap Quilt, 57" x 72"
Time—fast
Difficulty—easy

Yardage

Quilt top:

7/8 yard each of 5 different fabrics, progressing from dark to light

Border and Backing:

2 yards for inside border, 4-1/2 yards for outside border and backing.)

Recommended batting: See page 179.

Seam allowance: 1/4"

Strip width: 2"

Finished size of one rectangle: 1-1/2"

Finished size of one block: 7-1/2"

Blocks needed: 6 wide x 8 long = 48

1. Refer to the general instructions on working with Strips and Strata on page 82.

2. Cut the quilt top fabric into 2"-wide strips.

3. Sew the strips together in sets of five using a 1/4" seam. Always keep the same progression of dark to light—e.g., put the darkest fabric on the left. Otherwise you'll lose the distinctive pattern of Rail Fence or whatever pattern you choose.

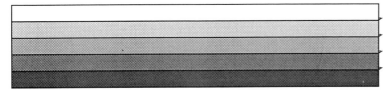

4. Press all seam allowances in the same direction.

5. Cut off a narrow strip to even up the fabric edge.

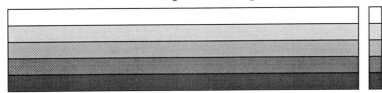

6. Cut crosswise every 8".

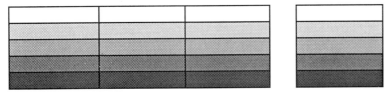

7. Arrange the finished blocks in a consistent pattern that pleases you. In this quilt, the light side alternates between being on top or to the left. See page 104 for variations.

8. Sew blocks together into rows.

> **"** I think Barbara Johannah's techniques have put quilts on more beds than would ever have made it if everything continued to be hand-pieced only. Because people could make quilts faster, they bought more fabric and helped to create a viable quilt industry. Fast machine piecing and machine quilting meant that you would be back at the quilt shop faster than if you had hand-pieced and hand-quilted the quilt.
>
> In the end, though, I think that technique is just a means to an end. Any technique that lets you make what your mind imagines is a good one. In that respect, Barbara opened up a whole new world for many quiltmakers. **"**

Doreen Speckmann, author
Pattern Play
Madison, WI

9. Press seams of all odd-numbered rows in one direction and seams of all even-numbered rows in the other direction: down, up, down, up, etc.

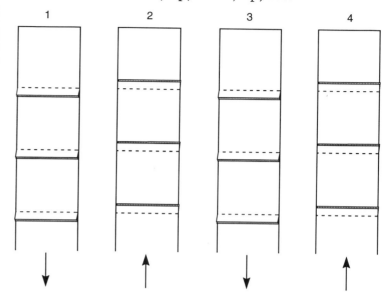

10. Sew rows together.

11. Press all final row seams in one direction.

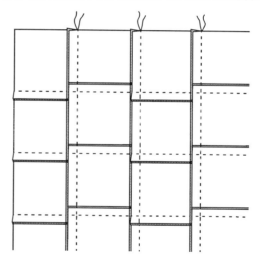

12. From each border fabric, cut off four long strips which are each 3-1/2" wide.

13. Sew one border strip to each side of the quilt top. Trim the excess off the ends of the strips.

14. Sew border strips to both the top and bottom. Trim the excess off the ends of the strips.

15. Repeat Steps 13 and 14 with the second border fabric.

Finishing

Use the Envelope Method on page 179.

Stitch-in-the-Ditch between the blocks is a good choice for this family of patterns. Because blocks are large (7-1/2"), most batting will require some interior quilting too.

Read Part Four: Machine Quilting for more information.

> **"** Abstract ideas are the patterns two or more memories have in common. They are born whenever someone realizes that similarity. . . Creative thinking may mean simply the realization that there's no particular virtue in doing things the way they always have been done. **"**
>
> Rudolf Flesch

Woven Rail

Magic Carpet

Aztec

Queen, 96" x 117"
Time—considering the number of pieces, not too bad
Difficulty—moderate

Rectangles: Log Cabin

I love the symbolism of this pattern. The rectangles of Log Cabin are the logs of the cabin. The square in the center represents the warmth of the fire in the hearth and is therefore traditionally red. Imagine you are above a log cabin and looking down its chimney.

The number and variety of sizes of the pieces in Log Cabin belies the ease and speed with which it can be made. There are no intersecting corners within the block so the blocks are quick and easy to make. The trick is to get the blocks to finish all the same size. There are so many seams that any errors build on themselves. Don't be overly concerned—just work carefully. Make extra blocks to allow for some that aren't quite the right size. This is a fun quilt to do.

Quick Quiltmaking transforms Log Cabin from among the slowest of quilts to among the fastest. Instead of cutting out small squares and rectangles for each block, you will speed-piece all blocks at once. This may be a new way of thinking about Log Cabin for you, so open your mind to the possibilities.

This setting is called Square Within a Square. Variations are shown on page 110.

Seam allowance: 1/4"
Finished size of strips: 1-1/2"
Width of strip: 2"
Finished size of blocks: 10-1/2"
Blocks needed: 8 wide x 10 long = 80

✎ Use scraps or small amounts of many fabrics. Alternately, combine positions on one side of the block into a single color. Yardage for the top is given by position. This is done to accommodate all of the variations possible with Log Cabin. Use only definitely light fabric for one side and definitely dark fabric for the other. Do not use fabrics that are in between. Your two sides must have strong contrast. Examples: light blues on one side and dark blues on the other, solid light pinks on one side and green prints on the other, or light earth colors on one side and dark earth colors on the other. Try a few ideas with colored pens. When you think you have your color scheme worked out, cut out a few snips of fabric. Pin them together. Are you getting the effect you want? Are you getting enough contrast? Experiment until you do. It really pays off with Log Cabin.

Yardage

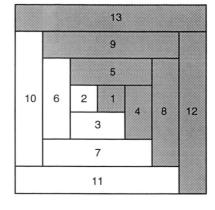

Quilt top:

Center
  #1. 3/8 yard

Light side
  #2. 3/8 yard
  #3. 5/8 yard
  #6. 3/4 yard
  #7. 7/8 yard
  #10. 1-1/8 yards
  #11. 1-1/4 yards

Dark side
  #4. 5/8 yard
  #5. 3/4 yard
  #8. 7/8 yard
  #9. 3-1/8 yards including inner border fabric
  #12. 1-1/4 yards
  #13. 3-5/8 yards including outer border fabric

Backing: 9 yards

Recommended batting: See page 179.

Making the Quilt Top

The block is numbered by the order in which it is put together. Starting with the center, #1, the pieces are added one at a time in a spiral. The spiral may be clockwise or counter-clockwise, but be consistent. One side is shaded to help you visualize what the block looks like.

1. Following the general instructions for making Strips and Strata on page 82, cut all of the strips 2" wide, cut on the lengthwise grain. First cut the border pieces from #9: 4 pieces 3-1/2" wide. Then cut #13: 4 pieces 4" wide. This one is cut wider to allow for turning to the back for a self binding.

2. Sew Strips #1 and #2 together in pairs along the right hand side, using 1/4" seams. Lay the pairs wrong side up on the ironing board, with Strip #2 on top. Open Strip #2 flat and press from the right side. Then close the strip.

3. Place several sets of strips on the cutting board. Cut crosswise every 2". You need a minimum of 80 combinations, but make more.

4. Again, press seam allowances away from Strip #1.

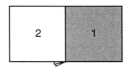

5. Place the combinations from Step #4 one at a time on a #3 strip, right sides together, with #2 always toward the top. Start the first combination about 1/2" down from the top edge of the strip. Place each succeeding combination aligned flush with the previous combination. The top edge of the second combination would just touch but not overlap the bottom edge of the first combination. Stitch along the right-hand side. Pinning is not necessary.

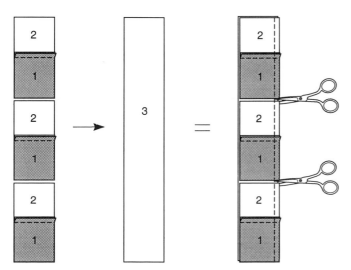

You will have to press combinations again later, but this initial pressing on long strips helps promote accuracy and prevents distortion.

Any error you make in not pressing seams fully open compounds throughout the block. That's why I like to make extras.

6. Using edges of the combinations as a guide, cut them apart. (You are cutting Strip #3 using the combination as a guide.)

7. Press seam allowances away from the center square #1.

8. Repeat Steps 5, 6, and 7 with each succeeding strip. Make sure your blocks are always growing in the same direction; either clockwise or counterclockwise is all right. What is important is continuing in the same direction once you have started. When you place the growing unit on a new strip, the last color pieced should be on top.

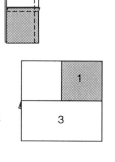

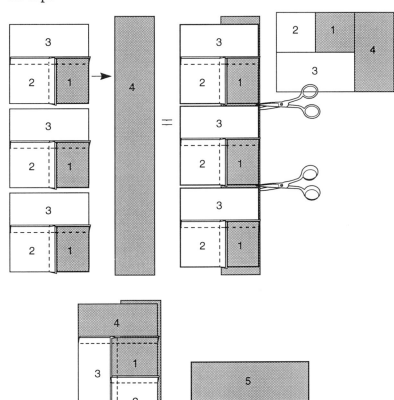

9. When you have more than 80 blocks made, measure each block. Each should be 11" square. You can either use a ruler to measure or make a paper or plastic template. If a block is too big, trim off up to 1/4". The blocks are big enough that you could also ease in one edge to another.

Use blocks that are too small in something else or appliqué them to the backing. It's easier to start over on one or two blocks than to fiddle making them fit. That's why I recommend always making 5% more than called for.

10. Lay out the blocks on your floor and try various settings (see page 110). Join the rows horizontally. Then join rows to form the quilt top. Add inner and outer borders.

Finishing

Either turn the outer-most border to the back for a self-binding or use the Envelope Method on page 179 with no binding.

Log Cabin is usually quilted Stitch-in-the-Ditch. For more information, read Part Four: Machine Quilting.

Courthouse Steps— The Other Log Cabin

Note that the piecing order of Courthouse Steps is different. Start from the center square and work out. Add pieces to opposite sides, in this case top and bottom, followed by left and right.

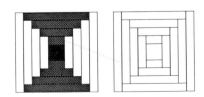

Cross Stitch

There is another alternative for finishing Log Cabins in addition to tying and quilting. It looks like a series of embroidered cross stitches.

Using pearl cotton (a crochet and embroidery thread), secure the thread on the back. Make a cross stitch through all three layers, finishing on the back. Take a back stitch to lock the cross stitch. Tunnel in the batting to where the next cross stitch is to be made. Come out on the back. (A pin pushed through from the front will accurately locate the spot.) Take a back stitch. Make another cross stitch and so on. The back stitches before and after each cross stitch are to secure the cross stitch and lock the tension between the cross stitch and the tunneling, the cross stitch having a firmer tension than the tunneling.

You can arrange blocks in lots of different ways. Don't be wedded to one arrangement before you start. Rearrange your blocks. Look. Rearrange. The setting arrangements given here are traditional ones, but there is no reason not to create your own.

In terms of setting arrangements, Log Cabin blocks with two adjacent sides dark and the other two light become subtle, rich, and complex Half-Square Triangle combinations. See Chapter 13, Designing Half-Square Triangle Quilts, on page 184. Then interpret the light/dark sequence with Log Cabin blocks. Here are three possibilities from one Half-Square Triangle design.

You can change the shape of the log-cabin block, thus the design of the quilt top, by changing the number of logs, width of the logs (they do not all have to be the same width), or the size of the center square.

Try these settings yourself.

Uneven width logs

Color reverse

Chapter 8. **Rectangles** | **111**

9.

45° Angles

While I am covering two kinds of quilts in this chapter, it is diamonds that I will discuss.

The blinders of tradition affect us all, I guess. We do most things the way we do because someone else taught us. It speeds up learning to take advantage of the discoveries of others. We would not get very far individually if we had to make every discovery on our own. However, that ready acceptance and faith in past knowledge can blind us to new discoveries. When the situation changes, do we continue to react in the ways that always worked before? Or do we reassess and make some new discoveries? There are so many things we accept without asking why.

It is hard to believe now that when I first developed the method for doing diamonds, I cut my strips on the bias because I had learned that diamonds must be on the bias. This was a great deal of additional work; it wasted fabric too. Later I tried making my strips on the straight grain of the fabric. This produced diamonds which have two sides on the straight and two sides on the bias. It not only works, but it works better with diamonds made from strips. The anticipated problems did not materialize. I came to the conclusion that at least with diamonds made from strips, there is no reason two sides cannot be on the straight grain.

You probably grasped quite quickly how strips are sewn into strata, and squares or rectangles are cut from strata. Diamonds cut from strata are a bit more difficult to imagine. Visually, the color sweeps one way, yet in construction, you work another direction.

Try thinking of diamonds as skewed or stretched-out-of-shape squares. The strips are staggered when sewn together and the strata cut at a 45° angle.

Greater skill is required of the sewer when working with diamonds, so if you are a novice, it would be wise to try squares first. A specialized plastic ruler cut at a 45° angle will facilitate the marking of the strata. You can also use a rectangular ruler with 45° lines printed on it.

45° Angles: The Star of Bethlehem

The Star of Bethlehem or Lone Star, as it is also known, consists of eight diamond arms. Using strips, you sew five different sequences of strata, each long enough for all eight arms.

Then you cut across the strata at a 45° angle, and assemble the five different slices into a diamond arm.

This quilt has such a strong design, I feel it looks best with something of interest around it, something as easy as using striped fabric, borders, additional piecing, or even appliqué.

Wallhanging, 60" x 60"

Time—very fast

Difficulty—most people find diamonds fairly difficult

Seam allowance: 1/4"

Finished size of unit: 2-1/2"

Width of strip: 3"

Finished size of arm along any side: 12-1/2"

Pieces needed: 25 per arm x 8 arms = 200

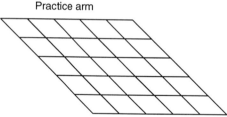 Yardage given by position of the numbers. Position is not the same as number of fabrics. You can have as few as two different fabrics or as many as nine.

Rows

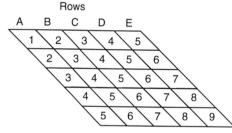

Practice arm

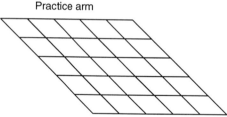 We are using five colors. That means Position 1 and Position 9 are the same color. So are 2 and 8, 3 and 7, and 4 and 6. Label your strips with their positions. (Post-It Notes are useful here.)

Our yardage:

First color: 1/4 yard

Second color: 1/2 yard

Third color: 2/3 yard

Fourth color: 3/4 yard

Fifth color: 1/2 yard

Yardage

Quilt top:

Position	Number of 3"x 45" Strips Needed	Your Color	Yardage
1	1		1/8 yd.
2	2		1/4
3	3		1/3
4	4		3/8
5	5		1/2
6	4		3/8
7	3		1/3
8	2		1/4
9	1		1/8

Background pieces, 4-5/8 yards

Helpful: Masking tape or Post-It Notes for labeling

Backing: 3-5/8 yards

Binding: 1 yard

Recommended batting: See page 179.

Making the Quilt Top

1. Following the general instructions for Strips and Strata on page 82, cut the fabric into 3"-wide strips.

2. Color the practice arm at left with your choices.

3. Start with Row A. Select one strip each of Positions 1 through 5. Using a 1/4" seam allowance, sew the strips together. For each new strip, stagger it about 2-1/2" below the previous strip.

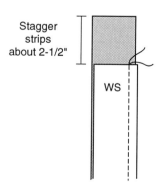

Stagger strips about 2-1/2"

WS

4. Use a plastic ruler that has a 45° diagonal line marked on it. Place the diagonal line of the ruler directly over one of the seam lines. Cut along the right ruler edge to trim off one staggered end. This establishes the baseline.

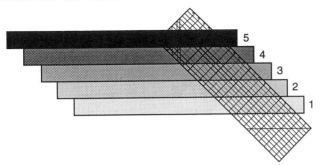

5. Turn the strata around.

6. Positioning the 45° diagonal line on the ruler exactly over a seam line, cut every 3" eight times. This gives you enough Row A's for all eight diamonds in the entire star.

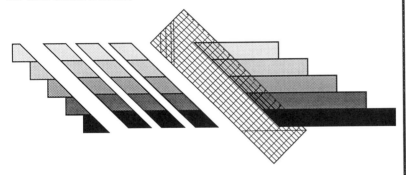

Recheck the positioning of the ruler each time you cut a slice. If the angle is off, you may occasionally need to cut a narrow pie-shaped wedge in order to maintain the proper angle for the diamonds.

Label these slices Row A (Post-It Notes again).

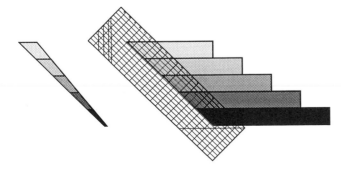

7. Repeat Steps 1 through 5 with Rows B through E, cutting eight slices for each row. Be sure to double-check positions and colors before cutting. Label the rows after cutting.

Blanche Young suggests placing a 45° angle template or ruler over the point of the diamond. If the diamond tip has become stretched, correct this by trimming. This should be necessary only at the tip.

8. Now sew Rows A through E together in order, to make a diamond arm. When sewing two rows together, the seams of the rows must intersect 1/4" in from the fabric edge, rather than at the fabric edges or the cross seams will not meet. Handle these edges carefully. They are bias edges and can easily stretch.

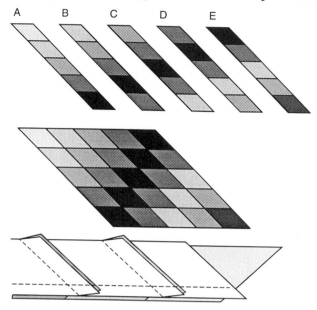

9. The eight large diamonds are now complete and ready to sew together. But first check the points of the diamonds to make sure they are true. Bias-cut fabric can stretch and distort out of shape. If this happens, the quilt will not lie flat, but will poke up in the center.

10. Sew large diamonds together into four pairs along the side with Positions 5 through 9. Start your seam 1/4" from the fabric edge and end your seam 1/4" short of the opposite fabric edge.

On the wrong side, the seam allowances will fan out in a circle. Press them flat. (If you sew all the way to the end of the diamond, you will have a layer of 16 seam allowances in one place. Sewing short of the edge and fanning out the seam allowances reduces the amount of bulk in one spot.)

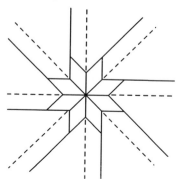

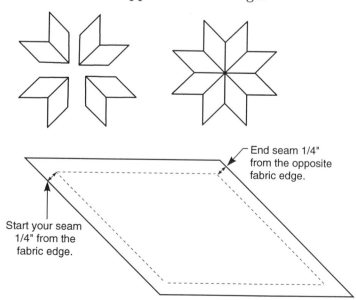

End seam 1/4" from the opposite fabric edge.

Start your seam 1/4" from the fabric edge.

| **Barbara Johannah's Crystal Piecing**

11. Sew the large diamond pairs together. I like to sew the upper pairs together and the lower pairs together, then sew the center horizontal seam. If you sew pairs together one after the other around the center, you may not like the look of your final star.

12. Do not cut out the background pieces until the star is finished. Then measure the side of the star (don't include seam allowances) to get the measurements needed for the background pieces. Cut a paper square to this dimension. Place the paper square on your fabric. Use a see-through ruler to cut four fabric squares, adding a 1/4" seam allowance on each side.

Now cut the paper square in half diagonally. Use one of the triangles as a template. Place the paper triangle on your fabric. Use a see-through ruler to cut four fabric triangles, adding a 1/4" seam allowance on each side.

This gives you a square wallhanging. If you want to make the quilt rectangular, add additional fabric to two opposite sides.

Finishing

Use Continuous Curve Quilting. Diamonds are just skewed squares. Continuous Curve Quilting is exactly the same for diamonds as it is for squares.

> ❝I consider Barbara Johannah the designer and originator of quick-piecing, strip-piecing techniques. Her first book revolutionized that part of quiltmaking and I don't think she is given credit for it nearly enough.
>
> A small bit in her first book was most helpful to me, although it was not repeated in the second one. For the Star of Bethlehem or Lone Star, using strip-piecing, she suggested cutting the fabric strips with the grain at a 22-1/2° angle rather than parallel to the edge of the board (drawing an angled line on the cutting board by which to align the cut). This made the strips a peculiar bias and allowed me to make a perfect miniaturized Lone Star that laid flat. Constructing it with ordinary strips had created a lumpy piece. This tip was probably left out of the second book because it was confusing to readers. I have had no difficulty in doing or teaching the normal strip-pieced Lone Star using straight- or crossgrain strips, but for small pieces I think this off-grain cutting method is well-worth considering again.❞
>
> Jane Hall, co-author
> *Precision Pieced Quilts Using the Foundation Method*
> Raleigh, NC

Any Size Star You Want

Jean Affleck, Pat Cairns' co-author on *Contemporary Quilting Techniques/A Modular Approach*, has worked out the math so we can easily plan large stars and speed-piece them.

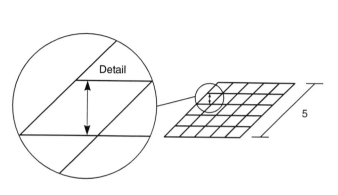

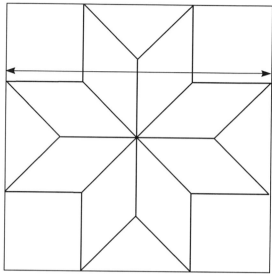

width of one finished diamond	times the number of diamonds across one arm of the star	the width of the star
	times the ratio 1 to 4.8 =	
Example:		
2.5"	x 5 =12.5 x 4.8 =	60"

You can, of course, start with the size star you'd like and divide backwards.

width of finished star

divided by 4.8

divided by the number of diamonds across one arm of the star =

width of one finished diamond

You can vary the number of diamonds and the finished width of the diamonds in the arm of the star. The important thing to remember is that the ratio of the arm of the star to the full star is approximately 4.8.

Increasing the Size

Measure the completed Star before cutting the borders. Remember to add seam allowances.

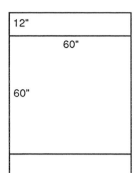

Twin
60" x 84"
Add 12" finished strips to top and bottom of Star.
You will need this fabric:
Border: 1-3/4 yards
Backing: 4-3/4 yards
Binding: 1 yard, 3"-wide continuous

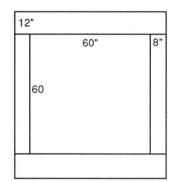

Double
76" x 84"
Add 8" finished strips to sides.
Add 12" finished strips to top and bottom of Star.
You will need this fabric:
Border: 2-1/2 yards
Backing: 5 yards
Binding: 1 yard, 3"-wide continuous

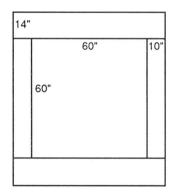

Queen
80" x 88"
Add 10" finished strips to sides.
Add 14" finished strips to top and bottom of Star.
You will need this fabric:
Border: 4-1/4 yards (fabric will be leftover)
Backing: 5-1/4 yards
Binding: 1 yard, 3"-wide continuous

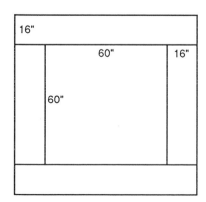

King
92" x 92"
Add 16" finished strips to sides.
Add 16" finished strips to top and bottom of Star.
You will need this fabric:
Border: 4-1/2 yards
Backing: 6 yards
Binding: 1-1/4 yards, 2-1/2"-wide continuous

45° Angles: King's X

This quilt is included with Diamonds rather than with the next section, Equilateral Triangles, because we are cutting 45° angles rather than 60° angles.

Generally, using a striped fabric means more work. Here, however, is a perfect pattern to combine with striped fabric.

Variations are shown on page 123.

King's X Block

Unit

Double, 76" x 95"
Time—average
Difficulty—average

Yardage

Quilt top:
 4-5/8 yards dark fabric
 4-5/8 yards light fabric

Backing: 5-1/2 yards

Binding: 1 yard

Recommended batting: See page 179.

Making the Quilt Top

1. For easier handling, cut each length of fabric into three equal pieces.

2. After reading the general instructions on Strips and Strata on page 82, cut each piece into 4"-wide strips.

Sew the strips together in pairs using a 1/4" seam allowance. Stagger the strips so that one strip is 3-1/2" lower than the other.

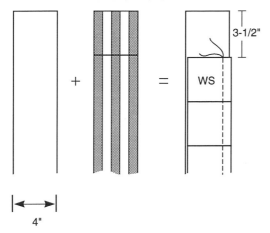

3. Press the seam allowances to one side.

4. Follow the intervals in the diagram for marking and cutting one strata into triangles. You may use a plastic ruler that is marked with a 45° diagonal line. Place the diagonal line of the ruler over the fabric edge or on the seam line. The edge of the ruler should now be at a 45° angle. Mark the strata into triangles.

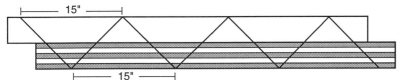

5. Cut on the lines you have marked.

6. Repeat with the rest of the strata. You should end up with more than 160 triangles, half with dark tips, half with light.

7. Spread 160 of the triangles out on a large table (e.g., ping-pong table) or on the floor. Experiment with them to see what designs you can come up with. Also look at page 123. Sketch your ideas on graph paper so you can easily compare them. The traditional King's X is made in blocks of four squares; each block composed of eight triangles.

Seam allowance: 1/4"
Finished size of unit: 9-1/2"
Width of strips: 4"
Units needed: 80
Blocks needed: 20
Finished size of block: 19"

✎ You will have enough extra combinations to make several pillows.

✎ You can combine marking and cutting by using a plastic ruler and a rotary cutter.

I prefer using my grid and straight edge, marking with a pencil, and cutting with scissors. I am more accurate that way. (See page 16 for a deeper discussion of my tools.)

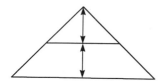

Use a 3/8" seam allowance to sew the triangles into squares along their longest side, pairing a light base with a dark base. Then use a 1/4" seam allowance to join the squares into blocks. Sew the blocks into the quilt top.

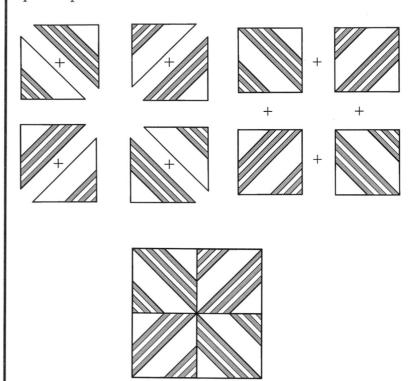

If you were to use a 1/4" seam allowance to sew the two combinations together, the finished width of the tip and base would not be equal. For patterns like King's X, where you sew units tip to tip or base to base, it may not matter.

For patterns where you sew units tip to base, an adjustment must be made. That's why you take a 3/8" seam allowance in joining triangles.

Finishing

Finish in the traditional way (see page 180). Bind, using a 3" strip. Quilt using Ernest Haight's Machine Quilting method. It will take two passes. Then do vertical and horizontal lines of Stitch-in-the-Ditch.

For more information, read Part Four: Machine Quilting.

Jane Warnick. See companion photo, elsewhere in color section. Both were developed from the Half-Square Triangle Element Key.

Harriet Hargrave, *Star Chain,* 68" square. One of the first quilts Harriet made with Continuous Curve Quilting and a darning foot.

Ernest B. Haight, *Butterflies* (see Chapter 11).

Nancy Brenan Daniel, *Mountain Zone Jazz,* 48" x 65". Nancy pieces strips, then cuts them in half the long way and moves the halves around.

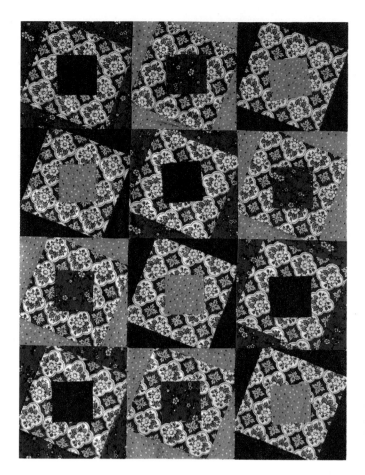

Marlene Andrey, 14" x 18⅝". Playing with Crystal-Pieced square grid and cutting the top layer only (see Chapter 5), Marlene fused extra fabric to the centers of the blocks.

Joyce Peaden, *Christian Cross*, photo by Photo Haus, Yakima, Wash.

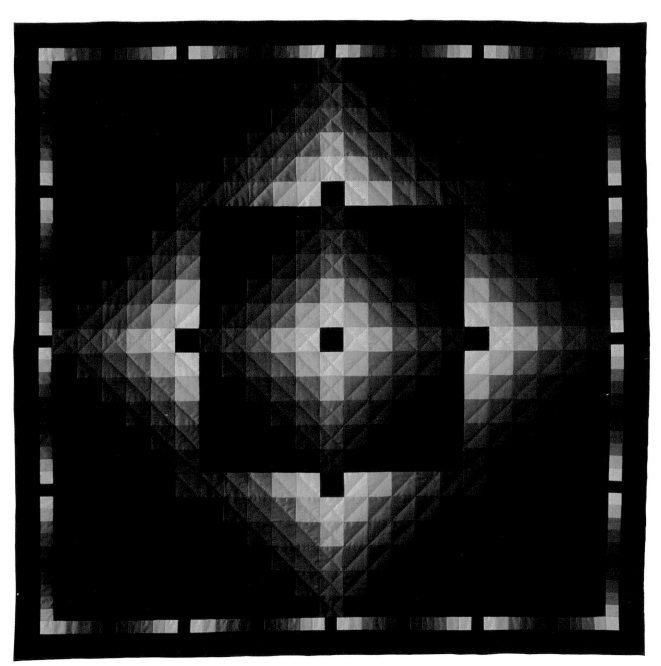

Lassie Wittman, untitled, photo by Ken Wagner

Left: Jane Hall, miniature *Star of Bethlehem;* started 15 years ago, the top one, pieced from crossgrain strips, would never lie flat. The bottom, pieced from slightly tilted grain (see tip in Chapter 9), was greatly improved.

Opposite: Anita Hallock, *Garden Path.* Reprinted with permission from *Scrap Quilts Using Fast Patch™* by Anita Hallock.

Below: Harriet Hargrave, *Lone Star.* Quilted with Continuous Curve Quilting on the star.

Bottom: Janet Elwin, *Goose in the Pond* detail

Sharon Hose, *Grandmother's Sky*, 46½" x 72". As with *Grandmother's Flower Garden*, this quilt uses some light tips, some dark tips (see Paired Quilts in Chapter 10).

Beckie Olson, *Log Cabin* (Barn Raising); quilted by Juanita Noel. Reprinted with permission from *Quilts by the Slice* by Beckie Olson.

Here are some other traditional patterns.

As you have noticed, the triangle combinations in King's X, Robbing Peter to Pay Paul, and Light & Dark are of two types—one dark-tipped, one light. The previous pattern used both types within each quilt. The following patterns each use just one of the types of combinations. To use up all of the combinations, you would need to make a pair of quilts. (See Paired Quilts on page 139.) One other possibility would be to use the second set of triangles for the backing and make a reversible quilt that resembles a woven counterpane quilt.

Robbing Peter to Pay Paul

Like King's X, this quilt pattern has even amounts of two colors. Adjacent blocks also reverse colors. Because of these two factors, the eye can't rest. The patterns are optical illusions, always changing. If you want to remove the optical illusion quality, make the quilt in more than two colors.

Light & Dark

Only use the 45° triangle method of making Light & Dark if you are using directional fabric like a stripe. If you are not using directional fabric, it would be faster to make this quilt strip-piecing four strips into strata, then cutting squares to make the basic unit. Of course, using a stripe makes this pattern more difficult because you must match stripes.

Xquisite

Xquisite uses just one of the two types of combinations. It can be worked with the tip color varied and the base remaining constant, or with the base color varied and the tip remaining constant, as in the illustration.

I wanted stars to show everywhere, so I extended tips into the borders. I used the dark-tipped unit combined with a plain triangle of background fabric.

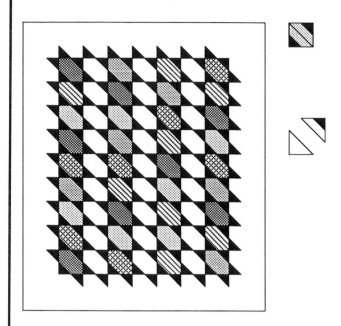

Grandmother's Own

This pattern could use the color reverses left over from the Xquisite. I used striped fabric in this example.

King's Cross Variation

This pattern is the same as Grandmother's Own, except that you use two different base color strips and keep the tip a constant color. You will have half the triangles left over for another quilt.

Star Cross

Like King's Cross, Star Cross uses a constant tip color and varies the base color. However, the choice of placement for light and dark is different. This is a good choice for a scrap quilt.

Governor's Palace Maze

Symbolism is possible in piecing, as well as in appliqué and quilting. The Governor was the King's man in Colonial Williamsburg. Therefore, when I designed this quilt, I used the King's X as a base. The four squares forming the King's X are in the center pivotal area.

The beauty of this quilt is enhanced if one of the fabrics is a stripe. The use of one striped fabric would have no effect on the level of difficulty of the King's X setting arrangement, but makes this one more difficult due to the necessity of matching the stripes.

Original designs such as Governor's Palace Maze may be more suitably assembled in rows, rather than in blocks, like King's X . As you sew, pick up only one row of squares. Using your drawing as a guide, sew them together. Return the completed row to the floor or table. Make certain you have the row assembled correctly. Pick up the second row and repeat the procedure. Sew the rows together into the quilt top.

Equilateral triangles haven't been explored much in machine piecing, although they offer vast possibilities for those who've tired of squares and the more common Half-Square Triangles. As always, you break down the visual pattern into components that you mass-produce.

Many quilters are now quite adept at seeing the Half-Square Triangle combinations within traditional piecing patterns. The same process is possible with equilateral triangles. You just need to get used to seeing a 60° grid in your mind's eye superimposed over these patterns. Soon you will be analyzing existing patterns and designing your own.

There are fewer 60° traditional quilt patterns than those that use 45° and 90°. I suggest several reasons for this. Working in 60° naturally produces equilateral triangles, 60° diamonds, hexagons, and half hexagons. When using templates, these shapes are cut whole. Consequently, seams are not straight-line sewing, but change direction constantly. This makes for beautiful patterns but more difficult sewing—hence fewer patterns have been developed.

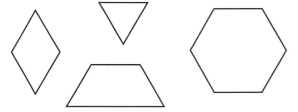

In my earlier books, I didn't want to deal with 60° either, simply because it wasn't easy to draw them. Then I discovered a tablet of graph paper at an art store with an equilateral grid on it (Alvin tablets—see also the back of this book for a grid). I began to play. Soon it became obvious that, using strip piecing, the patterns could be broken down into component equilateral triangles, which allows straight-seam sewing. Long straight-seam sewing as always is the key to efficient machine-piecing methods. If a pattern can be broken down into units that can be sewn in straight rows, it is a good candidate for machine piecing. Most 60° patterns break down easily into equilateral triangle components which can be sewn with long straight seams.

10. ◆
Equilateral Triangles

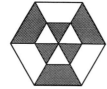

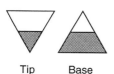

Tip   Base

Spider Web has four strips, not two.

Strip Method of Making Equilateral Triangles

As with King's X in the last chapter, basically you sew strips together into strata and then cut the strata apart. Instead of cutting at a 45° angle, we cut at a 60° angle to get equilateral triangles. Each strata produces two types of combinations, one with a light tip, one with a dark tip. The equilateral triangles are then sewn together into rows to form the patterns.

Spider Web, a traditional pattern, is given first, because I want to make a connection with what you already know. It is easy to learn to see the equilateral triangles within this quilt pattern. Then I'll show you less common designs and help you learn to see the equilateral triangle grid within all patterns like this. To simplify matters, all of the other patterns in this section are made with the same size triangle as Spider Web and are made from strata composed of just two strips (unlike Spider Web, which uses four strips). Keeping this part simple should open up possibilities for you.

When all the combinations are made from the same-sized triangle and from the same width of two strips, any combination can be used in any pattern. This is helpful as each strata produces two types of combinations, one with a light tip, one with a dark tip (see left). In this chapter I have designed some of the quilts to use both kinds. In others, a quilt that uses just one type is matched with another quilt that uses the other type—I call them Paired Quilts (see page 139). With some patterns, it isn't possible to use all of both types; if, however, you always work in a standard width of the initial strips, leftover triangle combinations are not wasted but added to a storehouse of ready-to-use combinations for future quilts. In this chapter, I'm using 2-1/2" strips.

Working with two even strips creates more possibilities than working with three or four strips or varying the width of the strips. The simpler something is, the more versatile it is as a unit for design.

This doesn't mean you should limit yourself to strata of two even-width strips. After you understand the method, vary the number and width of the strips. Varying the number and width of the strips will yield more contemporary patterns, while two even strips will yield more traditional patterns.

| Finished Size | | Strip Widths |
height	width	
2"	2-3/8"	1-1/2"
3"	3-1/2"	2"
4"	4-5/8"	2-1/2"
5"	5-3/4"	3"

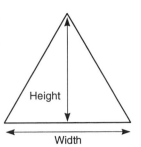

Understanding Why the Template Looks Funny

Before we make our first quilt, Spider Web, let's examine the nature of an equilateral triangle. It affects how we cut triangles. Not everybody understands that.

I recently received a promotional mailing for a new quilting book. A drawing and instructions were included on how to make a wall hanging of equilateral triangles. The instructions would never work, not even close, because sewing the triangle combinations to each other would result in strips of different width. We can blithely draw things on paper that will never work in fabric when we forget what taking a seam allowance does to the basic shape.

It isn't necessary to understand the following explanation to make equilateral triangle combinations. You can sew without understanding why. Just cut 2-1/2" strips and use the template included on page 134.

But for those who need to understand why, I hope the following explanation will prevent you from taking a shortcut and ending up with combinations that don't match.

So, here goes. An equilateral triangle has three sides of equal length. All three angles are 60°. Those angles must be accurate but there are other equally important measurements, if the triangle is pieced of strips. With most patterns, the strips within **the triangle must finish the same width** (see right column).

To achieve this, an adjustment needs to be made when cutting out the triangles. You can make the adjustment in one of two ways:

1. *Best way:* If you cut with a specialized equilateral triangle ruler or my template on page 134, the tip of the triangle has already been adjusted for you.

2. *Not-worth-it way:* If you cut with a plastic ruler with 60° lines on it, you will instead adjust the base of the triangle.

Tip With many geometric shapes, such as the square, finished quilts look essentially the same whether template-made or speed-pieced. Theoretically, any quilt can be made with template piecing, but many patterns aren't started because they're too difficult and more work than a quilter wants to do. Strip-pieced 60° patterns are not only faster than the template method, more important, they are easier. I expect the potential of 60° piecing patterns to be fully explored as quilters experiment with the strip method of making equilateral triangles.

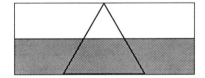

When a triangle cut like this is sewn to another triangle along the side, the top strip ends up narrower than the bottom strip.

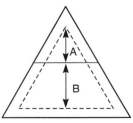

A does not equal B.

Chapter 10. **Equilateral Triangles** **129**

60° Triangle Ruler

This plastic tool is a hybrid of a ruler and a template. It works like a template but is multisized like a ruler. It's worth buying even if you make only one equilateral-triangle quilt. (Check with a quilt store.)

See also the template drawn on page 134.

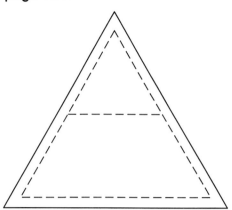

I've decided not to take valuable space explaining the second method. This is one time when a specialized ruler is definitely worth buying.

Best way: Marking the combinations with a specialized ruler or template

1. Follow the general instructions for making Strips and Strata on page 82.

2. Sew the strips together. Staggering them will save fabric. Press strips open.

3. Using the ruler or the template on page 134 as a guide, cut out the triangle combinations. Note that the triangle combinations are of two types and that the triangles have a truncated tip. Now the strips will finish an even width when you sew the triangles together.

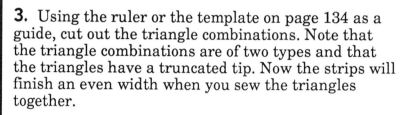

Equilateral Triangles: Spider Web

Spider Web uses both parts of the combinations—the light tip and the dark tip. This pattern has four strips in each strata. Cut combinations with a triangle template. (See page 134 for template.)

Queen, 83" x 103"

Time—more than average

Difficulty—difficult due to narrow pieces and many intersecting points

Yardage

Quilt top:

5 yards light fabric

5 yards dark fabric

2-1/2 yards for star points (could be light-colored or a third color)

Backing: 6 yards

Binding: 1 yard

Recommended batting: See page 179.

Seam allowance: 1/4"

Finished side of triangle: 4-5/8"

Width of strips for Spider Web: 1-1/2"

Width of strips for star points: 4-1/2"

Finished size of blocks: 9-1/4"

Number of blocks: 97 complete blocks and 26 partial blocks

Combinations needed: 690 triangles

Star points needed: 220

✏️ You must use a special triangle tool or make one using the template pattern on page 134.

Making the Quilt Top

1. First cut the star points. Follow the general instructions for making Strips and Strata on page 82. Make 4-1/2" wide strips. Use the template on page 134 to cut 220 star points.

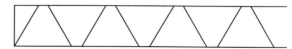

2. Now make the Spider Web blocks. Cut 1-1/2" wide strips from your two light and dark fabrics.

3. Sew the strips together into groups of four strips. Alternate light and dark colors.

4. Using the template on page 134 as a guide, cut the fabric into 690 triangle combinations.

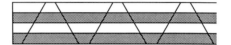

5. Separate the triangles into two stacks.

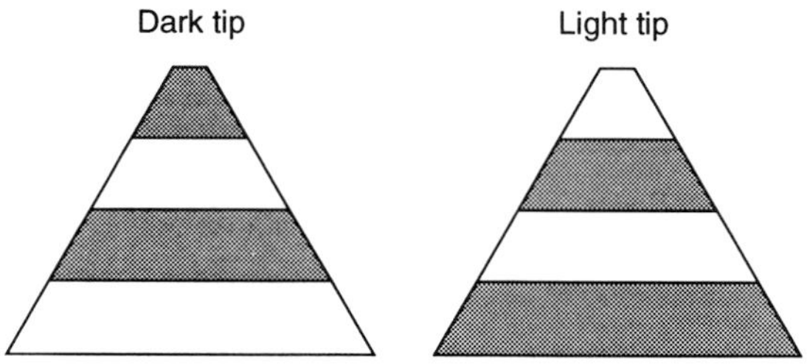

Dark tip   Light tip

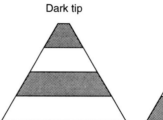

6. To make one Spider Web, sew six together, three from each stack. Alternate them so that every other one is light-tipped. Sew the top three first, then the bottom three. Then sew the horizontal seam. Press all seams in the same direction.

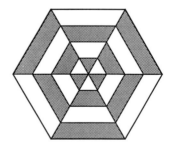

7. Sew two star points at opposite ends of the Spider Webs to complete the blocks. This is a complete Spider Web block.

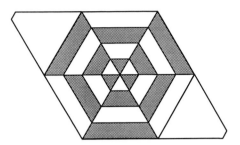

8. Sew the blocks together into rows following the instructions to the right for the number of partial blocks. Make sure the blocks are always turned in the same direction. The quilt is 13 rows tall. The ends of all rows need partial blocks, too.

9. Join the rows into the quilt top.

Finishing

Baste in the traditional method (see page 180). Stitch-in-the-Ditch on both sides of the basic units. Bind the edge with bias binding, cut 3" wide, following the contours of the Spider Web shape.

For more information, read Part Four: Machine Quilting.

Rows 1, 3, 5, 7, 9, 11, &13 need a partial block A

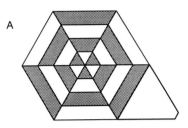

plus 7 complete blocks

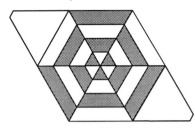

plus a partial block B

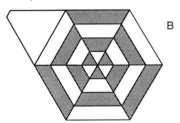

Rows 2, 4, 6, 8, 10, &12 need a partial Spider Web A

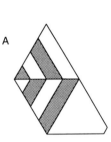

plus 8 complete blocks

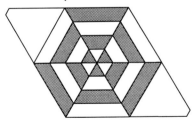

plus a partial Spider Web B

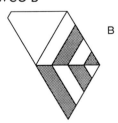

Template Pattern

The Star Points and the Spider Web sections must be cut exactly the same size as the pattern given here. (But it's much easier to buy a specialized 60° triangle ruler.)

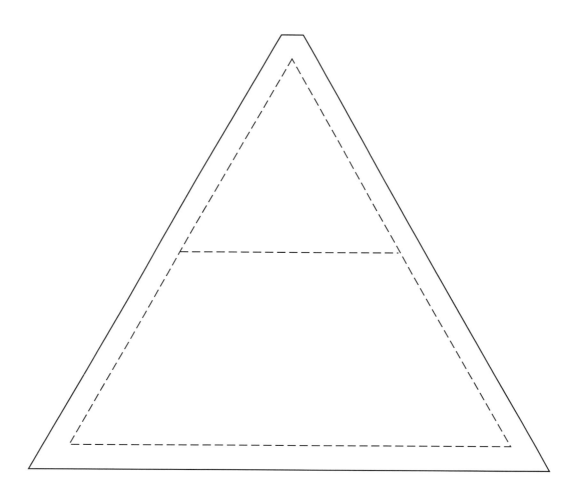

Twin, 61" x 84" (see diagram page 138)
Time—long
Difficulty—not for beginners

Yardage

Quilt top:

Fabric for flower petals and inner border of buds, 2 yards

Fabric for flower centers and outside row of border, 2 yards

(The flower petals could be made from scraps by making each strip for the strata 40" long. That's enough for one flower.)

Background fabric, 4-1/2 yards

Narrow borders: three straight-grain strips 1" wide x about 8' long and four strips 1-1/2" wide x about 8' long (will become self-binding).

Backing: 4 yards

Recommended batting: See page 179.

Equilateral Triangles: Grandmother's Flower Garden

Base   Tip

Do you remember that strip-pieced equilateral triangle combinations produce two types? This quilt uses both. The bases are used on the main area of the quilt and the tips are used in the border. Approximately the same number of each is needed, so it works out well, with few left over. Make extras. It is always easier to make a few extra in the beginning than to try to make more later or to adjust the size of those that don't quite fit.

The quilt is made in four sections— the main section and three border sections. Each section is made in rows. I've designed the background area to be made of whole triangles because I like the way it looks. You could combine some areas if you prefer.

This quilt gets hard only when you try to fit 60° angles into a 90° border.

Warning! The instructions for assembling this quilt are not for beginners. We'll show you the principles of the quilt, but we cannot explain every detail of putting it together, such as piecing where the buds meet in the middle, how to add the large white areas, and how to handle border corners.

Seam allowance: 1/4"

Finished side of triangle: 4-5/8"

Width of strips: 2-1/2"

Approximate size of flowers: 11"

Pieces needed:

A. 13 flowers x 12 triangles per flower = 156 combinations (78 light-tipped combinations of flower petal fabric and flower center fabric; 78 light-tipped combinations of flower petal fabric and background fabric)

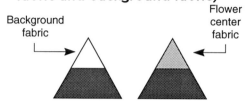

Background fabric

Flower center fabric

Flower petal base on both

B. 76 buds x 2 triangles per bud = 152 combinations (Use the dark-tipped set of triangles left over from the flowers.)

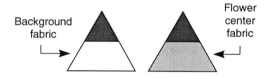

Background fabric

Flower center fabric

Flower petal tip on both

C. Approximate number of background triangles = 180

D. Fill-in pieces of the flower-center and background fabrics

Congratulations for finishing! This is one of the most difficult—and innovative—quilts in the book.

Making the Quilt Top

1. Follow the general instructions for making Strips and Strata (page 82) and equilateral-triangle combinations (page 127). Cut more than 13 2-1/2"-wide strips of flower petal fabric, flower center fabric, and background fabric. Make two sets of strata: flower petal/background and flower petal/flower center.

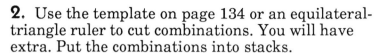

2. Use the template on page 134 or an equilateral-triangle ruler to cut combinations. You will have extra. Put the combinations into stacks.

3. Cut 4-1/2"-wide background fabric strips. These can either be cut into triangles and pieced to the flowers or left in long strips for piecing at the sides of the flowers (see diagram on page 137).

4. Make the main area of the quilt first. Following the diagram, sew the combinations and plain triangles into horizontal rows.

5. Now make the three narrow border sections. Piece the bud strips first. Where the buds meet, it's easier to take apart combinations that have already been sewn, adding a small triangle of color as needed, than to cut and piece the whole thing.

6. Place the bud strip on the sides and bottom of the main area. You don't have seam lines to align as you would on a 90° grid, so make visual decisions. You may want to elongate the top or bottom of the main area to make it longer before adding the border. Once you've decided, add background fabric to the border panels to give them the length they need.

7. Square up the main section. Sew on the inner narrow borders. Center the pieced borders on the main area and sew them on. Trim as needed.

Finishing

Sew on the outer narrow border and turn to the back as the binding.

For more information, read Part Four: Machine Quilting.

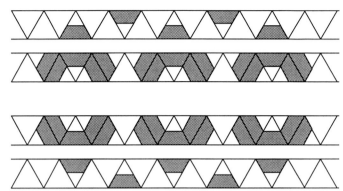

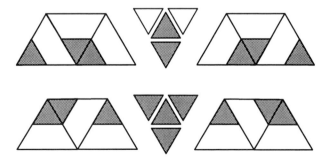

Detail of Center of Borders

Grandmother's Flower Garden

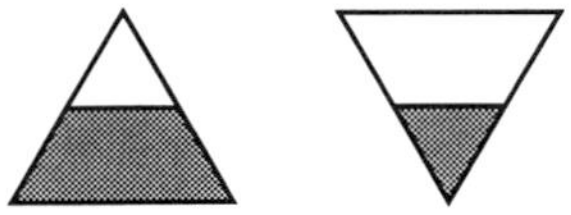

What Can Two Little Triangles Do?

Equilateral triangles made from strip piecing come in two types. Half have one fabric at the base and the other half have that same fabric at the tip. With some quilt patterns, such as Spider Web, both tip and base combinations can be used in the same quilt. Other patterns use just the tip or just the base combinations. When you use half the combinations in one quilt and half in another, I call them Paired Quilts. Paired quilts come from paired triangles.

This section doesn't have instructions on how to make a specific quilt. It's more of a documentation of quilt patterns in progress. I invite you to explore pleasing but simple patterns made with just the tip or just the base combination. At the end of the book is 60° graph paper. Copy it on a photocopier; then color in tips or bases and design your own Paired Quilts.

Equilateral Triangles: Paired Quilts

Light tip   Dark tip

“ Very early I knew that the only object in life was to grow. **”**

Margaret Fuller

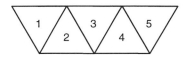

One row of triangles

Playing With Tips

Working with 60° graph paper, I colored in the tip half of each triangle. I worked with just dark and light and created this simple diamond and hexagon pattern. Train your eye to look at one horizontal gridline and one diagonal gridline of the underlying grid to find the combinations.

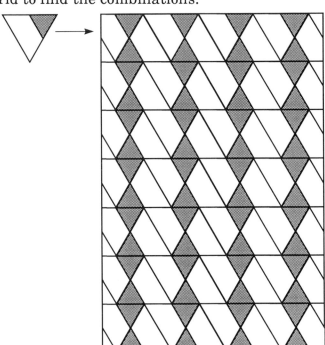

In the second design, tips create stars.

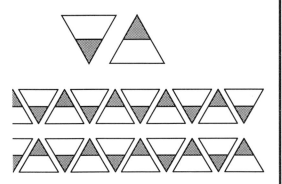

Playing With Bases

Now I've switched to playing just with the dark-base triangles. I shade in just the base portion of some triangles. Others I shade in completely or leave plain. I like these strings of stars and diamonds. These are designed in rows and would be sewn in horizontal rows.

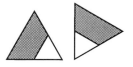

If you have trouble seeing the triangle combination, cut a piece of graph paper (see page 247), color in the base, and move it around on top of this design to find the basic unit.

Rather than designing in rows like the last pattern, next I designed a star within a hexagon to make one block. I shaded in just bases and didn't use any solid triangles. When I repeated the block four times it got a different look. These would be constructed in diagonal rows.

 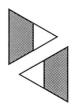

Triangle construction

What's the Best Construction Method?

After sketching these possibilities, I went back to the first quilt with light bases (page 140). I planned that these patterns would be made by sewing strips into strata, then cutting pairs of equilateral triangles, but was that really the best construction method?

Here's the pattern constructed by sewing together dark-tip triangles.

The pattern can also be constructed by strip piecing many long strips into strata, slicing across them, sewing the slices end to end, and sewing rows together to get the diamond shapes. Even though this pattern appears vertical, it is constructed on the diagonal. The final seam lines would run diagonally on the quilt. It would be easy to mismatch the rows so that they appear skewed.

Strip piecing with many strips is usually preferred over strip piecing with two strips and then cutting equilateral triangles, other things being equal, for its speed and on-grainline sewing. But I don't see one right answer here. Take your choice. Personally I lean toward sewing together the base-tip triangles rather than strip piecing as a construction method for this pattern, yet not using the strip-piecing method seems to require greater effort.

Strip construction

Adding a Third Color

Next I added a third color. I'm still using all dark tips, but now I've changed to two base colors. Two variations of the base-tip triangle must be made and this can't be strip-pieced. I had changed the parameters of the design problem I had given myself. How would adding a third color affect the other patterns I designed earlier?

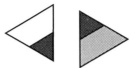

This is the pattern from page 140. Here individual stars stand out.

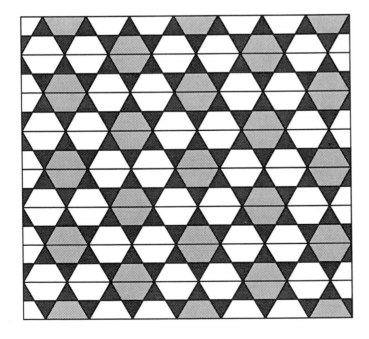

Both of these two patterns are the same basic block. Because a third color is used in different positions and the number of blocks is different, the two patterns appear different.

The bases are now dark and two colors are used for tips. The blocks are put in a different setting arrangement.

In examining designs, your eye is drawn to tips and sometimes it's hard to see the underlying grid. Look for three equilateral triangles of the same color under the tip. That's your basic combination.

Where does your eye rest? Our cultural upbringing determines what we see as the design and what area we see as the background. Look at one pair of blocks at a time. Within each pair, one block is the reverse coloration of the other. In each block do you see the black or the white as the pattern? Do you see the connected pieces or the isolated pieces as the pattern?

Here's a pop quiz. Can you figure out how to make this quilt, designed by Rosalyn Carson and called Synchronized Snakes?

Barbara Johannah's Crystal Piecing

Part Four:

Machine Quilting

As much as we'd like to, it is not practical to hand quilt every top, especially if it is a top we have made quickly. Is it appropriate to spend more than 100 hours on quilting a top pieced in ten? Sometimes, yes; more often, no.

Sometimes our choice is not between a hand-quilted quilt and a machine-quilted quilt, but between a machine-quilted quilt and no quilt at all.

Machine quilting gives you the textural beauty of hand quilting but in a much shorter time.

This chapter explores three ways to quilt with a presser foot on.

11.

Machine Quilting Three Ways

The Old Way

I always hated "machine quilting," those wavy lines of commercial machine quilting that obscured the piecing and made the quilt look like pre-quilted material or mattress pads.

No wonder it has never caught on! It is fast all right, but to my way of thinking, you ruin the beauty of the piecing.

As an alternative, sometimes the machine is used to mimic hand quilting. Each piece to be quilted is quilted individually. This requires a lot of starting and stopping. It also presents the problem of securing the beginning and ending of your stitching lines.

To secure the ends with this method, many quilters sew in one spot. This gives a slight thickening to the beginning and ending stitches.

Another alternative is to pull all of the beginning and ending threads to the back. The result will look fine on the front. But the back is a nightmare of threads to finish off. There goes much of your hoped-for speed.

These approaches to machine quilting point out two important attributes of *successful* machine quilting:

1. Continuous stitching lines and

2. A minimum of starts and stops so there will be fewer threads to finish.

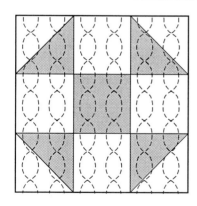

The old machine quilting

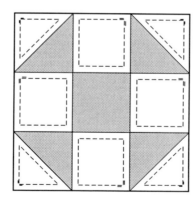

The stop-and-start method leaves...

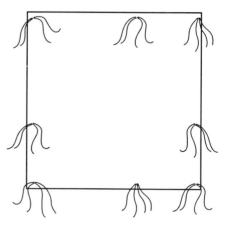

. . . too many ends on the back.

To be esthetic, quilting must either visually reinforce the piecing design or provide an independent but complementary design. By quilting some areas and not others, you push the quilted areas down, giving the piecing a third dimensionality.

New Ways

Wanting to finish all those quilt tops I had gleefully speed-pieced, I began to look for ways to meet the demands of the sewing machine with the bulk of a quilt. I had to consider these points.

Aims:

1. Minimizing the number of starts and stops.
2. Continuous stitching lines.

Limits:

1. The amount of fabric and batting that will fit under the arm of the sewing machine and can be easily turned.
2. Mistakes are not easily ripped out.

I find three methods to be appropriate:

1. Stitch-in-the-Ditch
2. Ernest Haight Machine-Quilting Method
3. Continuous Curve Quilting

Let's look at each method.

1. Stitch-in-the-Ditch

Stitch-in-the-Ditch entails quilting over seam lines. Generally you quilt in major seam lines, trying for long, straight seams. Hold the fabric on either side of the seam open as you sew. When you let go, the quilting line will be buried under the slight fold of the fabric. If done well, Stitch-in-the-Ditch doesn't show.

If you know you will machine quilt with this method, be sure to press seams to one side when you piece. A pressed-open seam which is later quilted by Stitch-in-the-Ditch may break or allow batting to escape.

Stitch-in-the-Ditch has minimal starts and stops and continuous seams, but it does not enhance the quilt as much as other methods. It's purely functional, holding the layers together.

One by one, the branches of quiltmaking are becoming integrated with the sewing machine—appliqué, piecing, and finally quilting. While demonstrating at quilt shows, I've watched the evolution of acceptance of machine work go from "It's not the right way" to "It works, but the workmanship isn't as good" to "Of course, how else would you do it?" Someday we'll be wondering what all of the fuss was about.

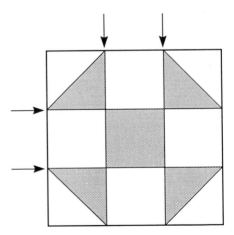

"In 1987 I went to work for a quilt magazine publisher as an illustrator/designer and discovered quilting. I immediately read everything I could in their extensive library. Reading about techniques quickly became my favorite kind of quilt reading, since I believe that each time you understand another good technique, it gives you that much more creative freedom.

Since I didn't know much about quilting, my selections were arbitrary. Lady Luck was with me, because a couple of Barbara Johannah's books were among the first books I chose to read. What she said made so much sense, it didn't occur to me that she was revolutionary. Then as I began to read other books, patterns, and directions, I would wonder, "Why in the world do they do it *that* way?"

Looking back, I was so naive. I didn't even realize that machine quilting wasn't widely accepted, and that even machine piecing still had a few detractors.

Among staunch traditionalists, Barbara's books must have read like Karl Marx's.

Since then, I have read many books and articles on new ideas and techniques. I believe many of the really good ideas were planted deeply several years ago by Barbara Johannah. They have become so much a part of our thinking that often we aren't even aware of where they came from. She planted seeds that have brought in a magnificent harvest."

Hari Walner, Designer/Owner
Beautiful Publications
Thornton, CO

2. Ernest Haight Machine-Quilting Method

Like me, Ernest B. Haight of David City, NE, experienced the pile-up of pieced tops waiting to be quilted. His approach to this dilemma was completely different from mine. Consequently we machine quilters have another option.

Mr. Haight's practical mind wanted a method that satisfied these criteria:

1. Fast straight-line sewing.
2. Sewing only on the diagonal (bias)—the slight stretch of the fabric would help keep the top and bottom flat and wrinkle-free.
3. Sewing with most of the quilt to the left of the sewing machine and the lesser amount under the arm of the sewing machine.
4. And of course, a minimum of starts and stops.

In the simplified diagram given here, the quilting lines would be about 2-1/4" apart on a 40" x 48" quilt. If you want the quilting lines to be closer together or if you want a larger quilt, you must add additional quilting lines between those given in the diagram (see discussion on page 156).

Examine the diagram to comprehend the practical simplicity of Ernest Haight's Machine-Quilting Method.

Starting at the corner marked A, you sew diagonally until you come to the opposite edge of the quilt. Pivot and sew diagonally again. At the end of this second seam pivot and sew a third diagonal seam. Continue sewing as you ricochet off the sides of the quilt until you can go nowhere else with this seam.

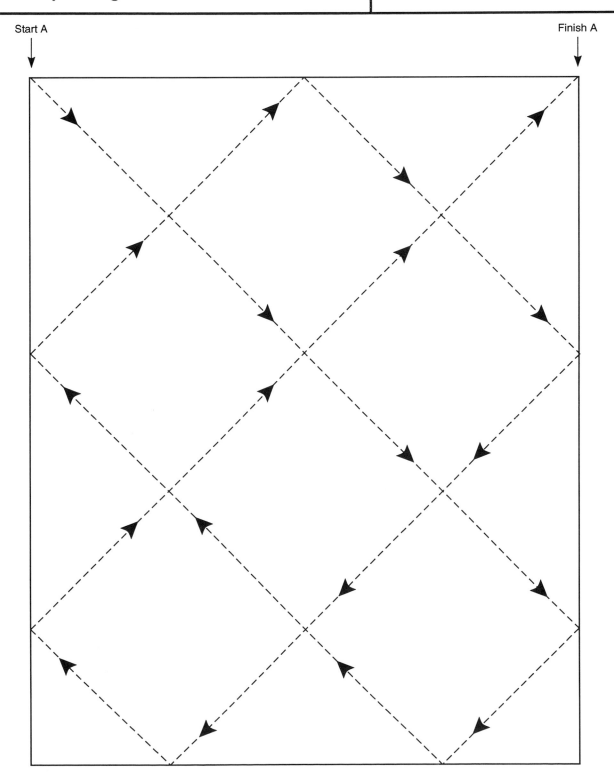

Finish B

Start B

This drawing shows three completed seams. Notice where C finishes. Can you see why you don't pivot again and continue sewing? Mr. Haight stops here because if he didn't, almost the entire quilt would be under the arm of the sewing machine on the next pass. You will get that seam done later with only the tip of the quilt under the arm of the machine.

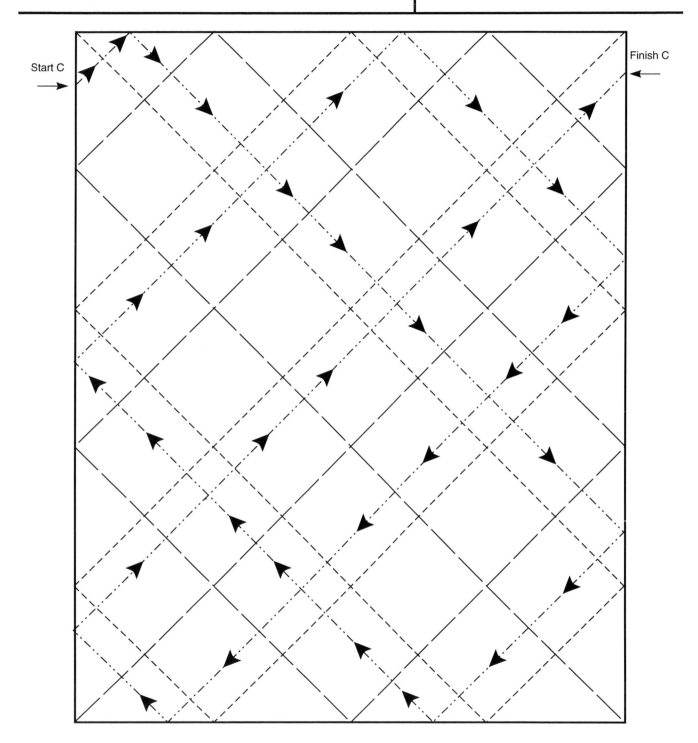

Start C

Finish C

Here's the final diagram for this quilt.

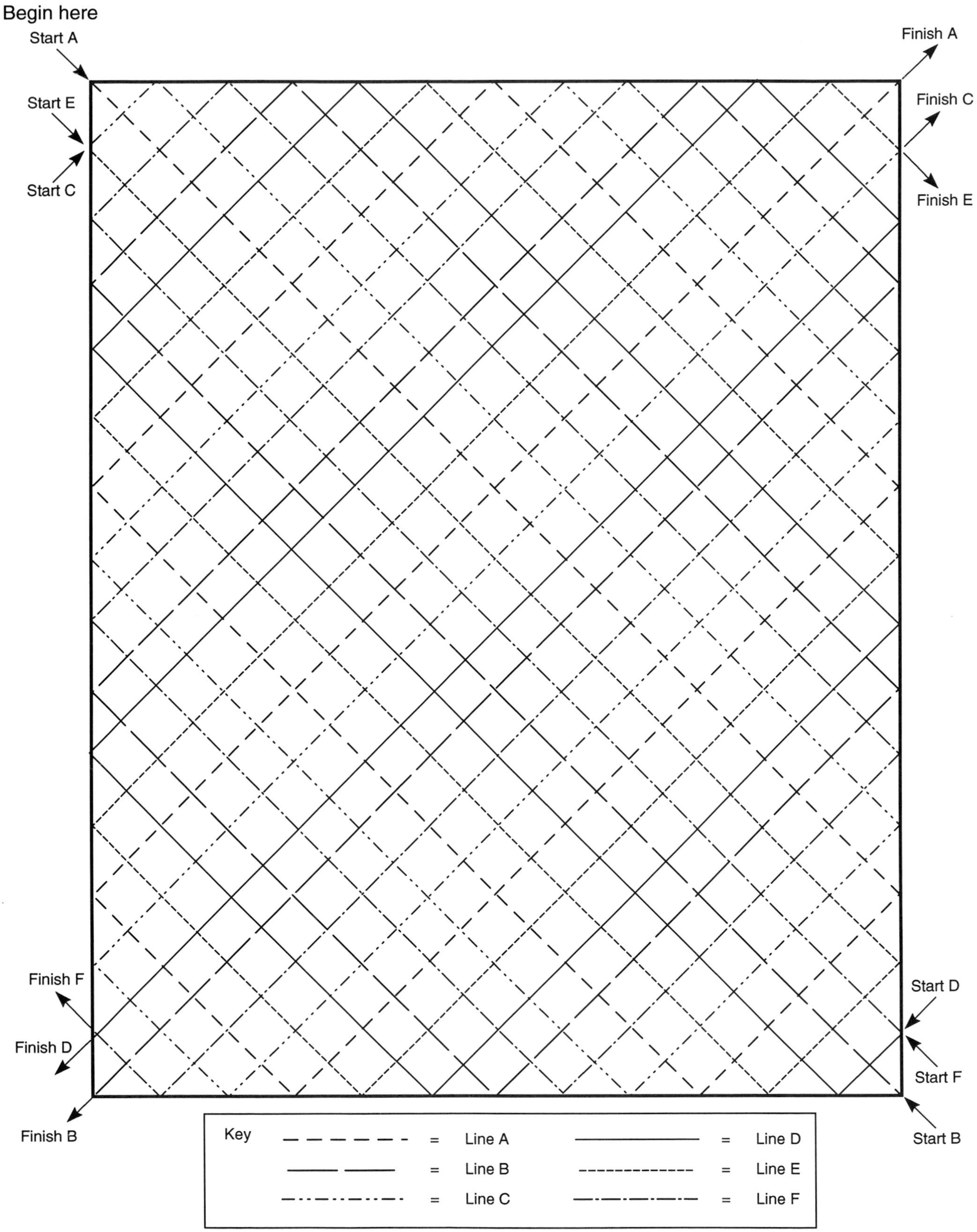

Begin here
Start A
Finish A
Start E
Finish C
Start C
Finish E
Finish F
Start D
Finish D
Start F
Finish B
Start B
Key
= Line A
= Line D
= Line B
= Line E
= Line C
= Line F

Haight's Ratios

Certain ratios of height to width work perfectly with Ernest Haight's quilting method. In the first example given on page 156, the ratio of the width to the height is 12 to 15 or 4 to 5. Other ratios will work as well (see below).

If your quilt top is not in these proportions and you want to use Ernest Haight's method, you may want to add borders to make the quilt perfectly proportional.

You can of course use this method on any size quilt, but you won't get the perfect ricochet and you will have to add more lines of quilting than you realize. Obviously, every additional line of quilting takes more time. Also, too many lines of quilting are unattractive.

Table of Ratios

Possible Ratios	Possible Quilt Sizes
4 to 5	4' x 5', 6' x 7-1/2', 8' x 10'
3 to 4	1-1/2' x 2', 3' x 4', 4-1/2' x 6', 6' x 8'
7 to 9	3-1/2' x 4-1/2', 7' x 9'

Planning the quilting design

Before you use Ernest Haight's Machine-Quilting Method, make sure your quilt design is appropriate. The best candidates are quilts whose patterns are on a 90° grid. In other words, quilts made of squares, rectangles, and Half- and Quarter-Square Triangles. It can also work well on 60° grid patterns.

Once you have a quilt design, sketch it on graph paper. Paper-clip a piece of tracing paper over your quilt design. Draw quilting lines on the tracing paper. In this way you can try a different quilting path with each piece of tracing paper without the need for resketching your quilt design.

✎ Note that with this pattern most of the quilting lines are in the ditch and the remainder bisect the piecing.

Barbara Johannah's Crystal Piecing

On quilts based on 45° and 90° grids, the quilting lines can enhance the piecing design. With some patterns, marking the quilting lines is even unnecessary.

However, true star patterns such as the Star of Bethlehem would not be enhanced esthetically by Mr. Haight's method, although the quilting would still be fast and functional.

So again, this method is best for simple repetitive patterns composed of squares, rectangles, and Half- and Quarter-Square Triangles and some 60° patterns.

The following illustration is not a sampler quilt. It shows a variety of blocks with the machine-quilting grid superimposed. Decide for yourself which blocks look good, which, not so good.

Square Quilts

Ernest Haight's method can be used with square quilts as well. There will simply be more starting and stopping and less ricocheting off of the sides, but it really works just as easily.

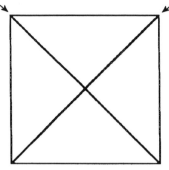

1. Sew an X.

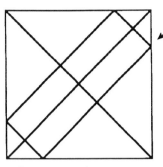

2. Sew a rectangle.

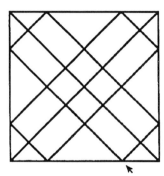

3. Sew a second rectangle.

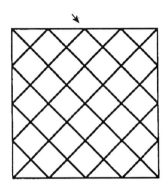

4. Fill in with a square. Add as many additional rectangles as you like to get the desired spacing of the quilting lines.

What if you want to start the quilting line one increment over from the corner? It's okay. You don't need to start at the corner. Let your design determine whether you start in the corner or one increment over.

What if you want close quilting lines? You can sew between the first set of quilting lines, consequently doubling the amount of quilting, but you may discover that the quilting lines distract from your piecing pattern rather than enhancing it or being neutral. Check the results before stitching by making a paper mock-up of one block and drawing the quilting lines on it. Do you like the looks? Does it look too much like a mattress pad? If this is the case, choose another method of quilting.

First option.

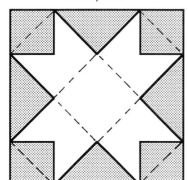

Moved over one unit.

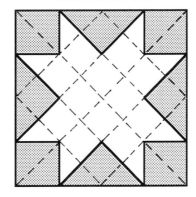

Use both for double the amount of quilting.

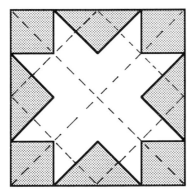

Saw Tooth Star

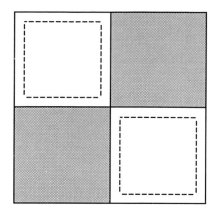

3. Continuous Curve Quilting

Continuous Curve Quilting is a method of machine quilting pieced patterns which is adapted to the unique attributes of sewing machines. It is the sewing machine equivalent of hand quilting. You quilt in the area that you want to and then move easily to the next areas to be quilted without finishing off and beginning new threads. You accomplish this by quilting in gentle arcs going through the corners to reach the next area to be quilted. This minimizes the number of starts and stops. It is esthetic as well as functional quilting, in that the background is quilted and the design is not, giving a three-dimensional effect.

Continuous Curve Quilting satisfies all of the desired goals. It has minimal starts and stops, continuous seams, and visual reinforcement of your piecing.

Before showing you how, look at this simple four-patch. It is quilted in the traditional way. Each shape you quilt is quilted independently. This is no problem if you quilt by hand. You simply quilt one square and then tunnel between the layers until you get to the next space you want to quilt. Sewing machines, obviously, can't do this. This, and the fact that you can't take advantage of the sewing machine's speed, are the primary reasons why sewing machines need methods of quilting designed specifically for sewing machines.

So how do you quilt both squares with one start and stop?

Go through the corners!

Start at an outside edge. Quilt in gentle arcs following the sides. Go through the corners to reach the next area to be quilted. Note that the quilting order is different from hand quilting. You don't complete one area of the background and move to another. Instead you stitch through the corner that connects one area of background to another. Eventually you return to where you started and complete the first block. This usually allows you to quilt with one start and one stop.

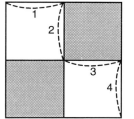 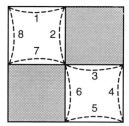

Barbara Johannah's Crystal Piecing

Here are the guidelines:

1. Plan a quilting path to cover every area you wish to be quilted.

2. Don't stitch over any quilting line more than once.

3. Try for one start and one stop. (It is not always possible or desirable.)

To do it:

Put your pencil point at an outside seam.

Following the rules, draw in all of your quilting lines without lifting your pencil until you are through.

It may take you a try or two before you figure out the best path. Other patterns can be worked following many different pathways.

Here's a simple pattern to practice on. You might photocopy it several times and try different paths.

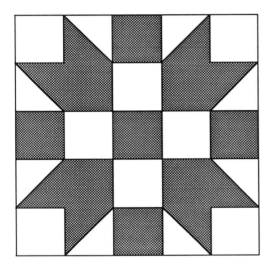

It's not the distance from the seam; it's not whether you're working on light or dark—it's going through the corners that is the key.

You can sew with the seamline either to the right or left of the presser foot. Or if you are adept at free-machine quilting, all of this becomes a cinch.

Here's one way to quilt it with Continuous Curve Quilting.

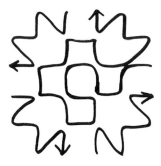

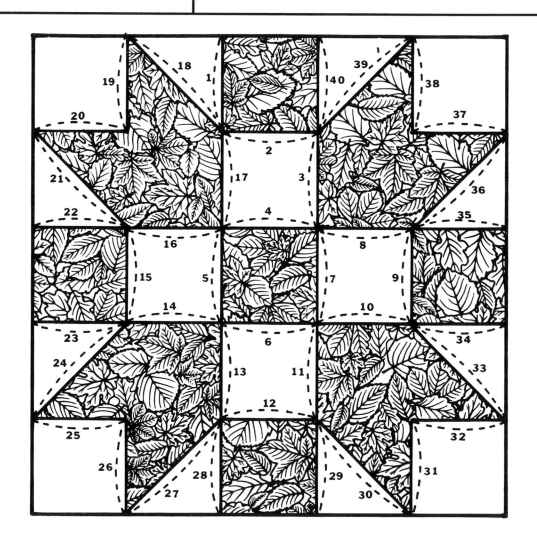

Barbara Johannah's Crystal Piecing

When to Use Continuous Curve Quilting

Continuous Curve Quilting is ideal for patterns in which some of the pieces form a design and you perceive the rest of the pieces as a background. I call this a figure/background relationship. For these patterns you want the part you see as the design (the figure) to come forward and the part you perceive as the background to visually recede. To get this three-dimensional effect, quilt only the background.

Some patterns do not have a figure/background relationship or they may have only a weak one. This is generally a result of color choices. Patterns done in a rainbow effect or differing values of a single color will not have a figure/background relationship. Sunshine and Shadow, Trip Around the World, and Star of Bethlehem are examples of quilts where colors often blend rather than contrast. With these patterns, the quilting is primarily functional rather than esthetic, so Stitch-in-the-Ditch and Ernest Haight's Machine-Quilting Method may be more appropriate.

Let's analyze some patterns appropriate for Continuous Curve Quilting. Remember in all of these, there is no one right way to proceed. If you don't like my way, devise your own.

Analyzing Patterns

The sequence of Continuous Curve Quilting falls into rough categories. (Please invent your own categories!) These diagrams give you an overview of the general quilting sequence. Later, we'll look in detail at some traditional patterns.

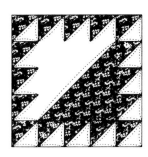

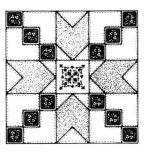

I sew on an old machine that moves the fabric. That's why I strip-piece each row in opposite directions and why I quilt in opposite directions. If you have a newer machine or use a walking foot, this is not necessary.

Silhouette

In very simple blocks, you merely quilt around the outside edge of the pattern. Also quilt around the outside edge of the entire block if you wish. (You may also want to use a different quilting method in the center of the star. Continuous Curve Quilting combines nicely with all machine-quilting techniques, including free-machine quilting.)

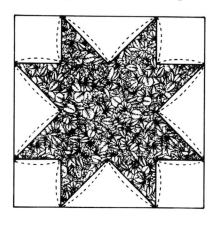
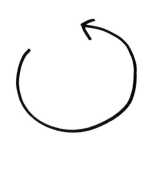

Isolation

Some patterns have isolated areas. Here, I'd start in the center and quilt. I like to work the center areas as early as possible. Then I'd move to the outer area.

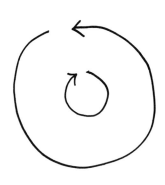

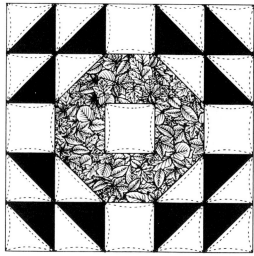

Barbara Johannah's Crystal Piecing

Rows

Some are done in rows.

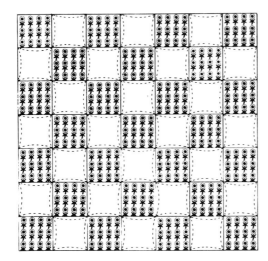

In and Out

With many patterns, you start at the edge and go into the center. You then quilt out and in, one-quarter at a time.

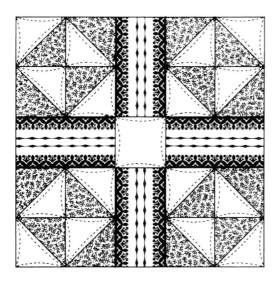

Remember, these are bird's-eye views of the quilting. Within each section, you will make many loops—see details later in the chapter.

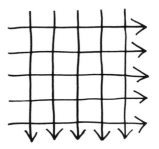

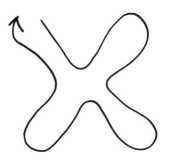

Spiral

More complicated patterns are often done in a spiral. You start at the edge and go in to the center. You then quilt in an ever-widening spiral. When I see a complex pattern with rings of design which go out from the center, it says to me, "Use a spiral." Once again, I like to get into the center as quickly as possible and quilt outward.

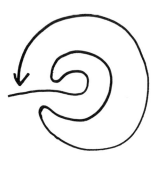

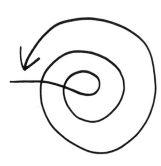

Diagonal

Patterns where blocks are set continuously should often be quilted diagonally.

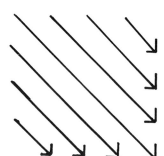

Analyzing a pattern to see if you can categorize it will make the actual work at the machine a lot easier. The quilting sequence is often obvious enough when you look at a block flat on the table, but a bit more elusive when you are actually sewing on it.

Having categorized a pattern will give you a general guide to follow. You may find it unnecessary to either follow a numbered guide or to number your block. What if you do get off the track and quilt out of sequence? It certainly does not make any difference in the end result. It just means you may have an additional start and stop or two.

Problem patterns

Watch out for some figure/ground patterns which are not suitable for Continuous Curve Quilting.

One of these is when the background areas to be quilted are isolated from each other. In the Cats and Mice example you can't get directly from one quilting area to the next. This pattern is a good candidate for Stitch-in-the-Ditch. (Of course, you could always quilt the figure areas instead.)

This Star is not suitable for an entirely different reason. Doing Continuous Curve Quilting would result in the intersection of 16 quilting lines. Too many! The block would not lie flat.

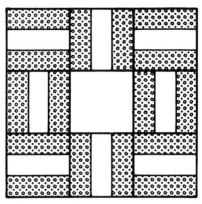
Cats and Mice

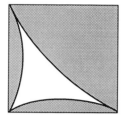

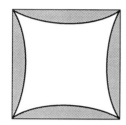

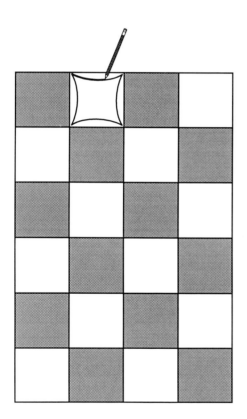

Marking the Quilt Top

You have the choice of 1) making a template and marking the quilting lines or 2) quilting by eye. In addition to your level of skill and degree of confidence, consider how much the quilting will show once completed. On a solid, I mark the quilting lines; on a busy print, I do it by eye. Try it both ways and make your own decision. If you choose to mark the fabric, here's how.

Templates

You could mark the quilt top free-hand, but for greatest precision, make a template to mark the quilting lines.

Trace the shapes in your quilt top—square, triangle, rectangle. Then draw a line that gently arcs in the center of each side. Make the arc proportional to the size of the block. It doesn't have to be 1/4" or 1/8" or any fractional inch from the seamline. (Patterns for many sizes of templates are provided in my book *Continuous Curve Quilting.*)

Glue the templates to plastic, acetate, or a bacon package liner and cut out. (You may peel off the paper once the template is cut out if you wish.) Plastic or any material that will take and keep a sharp point is required. Tag board, cardboard, sandpaper, etc., will not work.

Place the template on the piecing and draw around it with the marker you have previously tested for removability. Before marking your pieced work, please make sure the marks will come off after quilting.

Barbara Johannah's Crystal Piecing

Continuous Curve Quilting Patterns

Suggested sequences to quilt some well-known patterns follow.

Is this the only sequence?

No. Most of these can be quilted in many different sequences to achieve the identical end result. If you don't quilt the curves in the order I have given, it does not make any difference in the end result. I have given the sequence that seems most logical to me. You may find another sequence is easier for you.

If you have a quilt top on which a three-dimensional effect is not important, you may want to Stitch-in-the-Ditch instead of using Continuous Curve Quilting. Most of these sequences work just as well for Stitch-in-the-Ditch. In fact many patterns lend themselves to a combination of the two. Regardless of whether you choose to do Continuous Curve Quilting, Stitch-in-the-Ditch, or Ernest Haight's Machine-Quilting Method, you will still follow the basic concept:

1. Reduce the number of starts and stops.

2. Stitch continuously as much as possible.

3. Go through the corners.

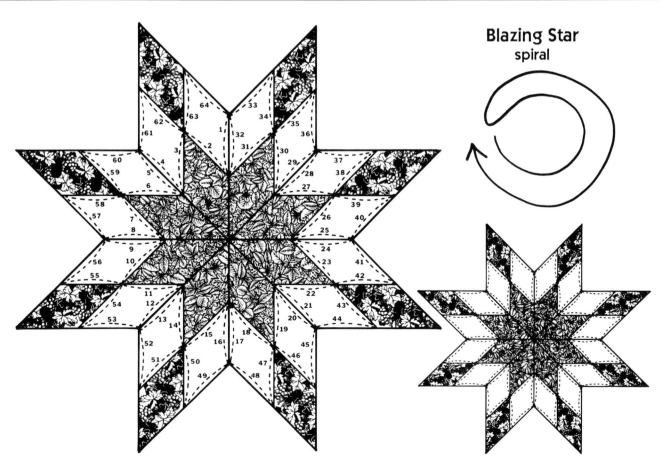

Blazing Star
spiral

Checkerboard
rows

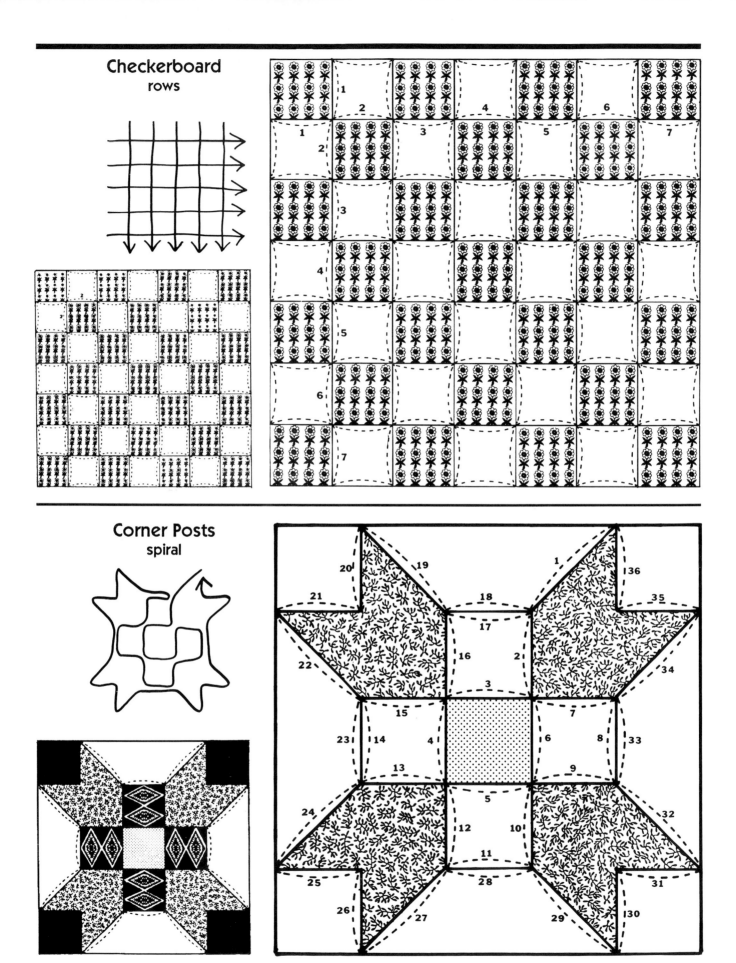

Corner Posts
spiral

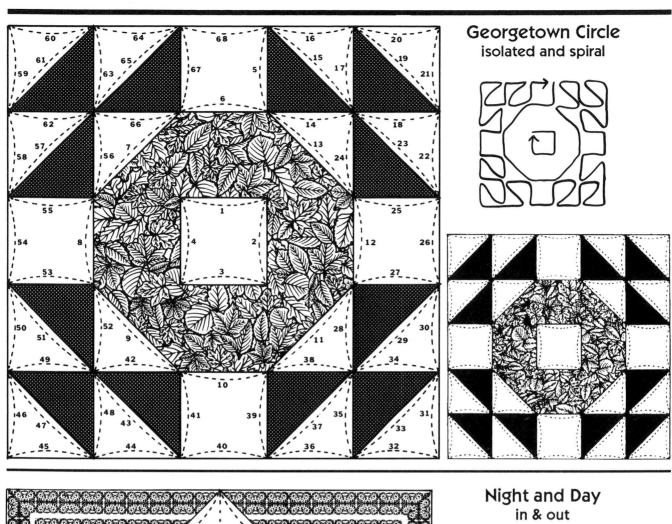

Georgetown Circle
isolated and spiral

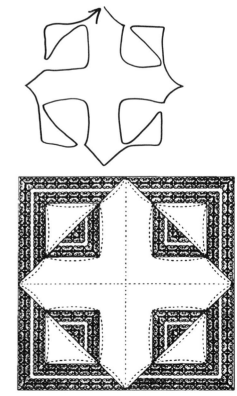

Night and Day
in & out

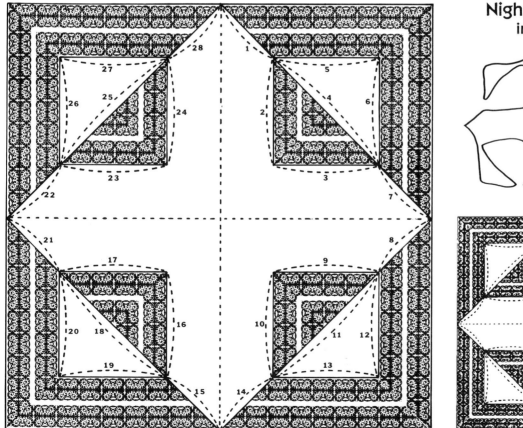

Chapter 11. **Machine Quilting** **171**

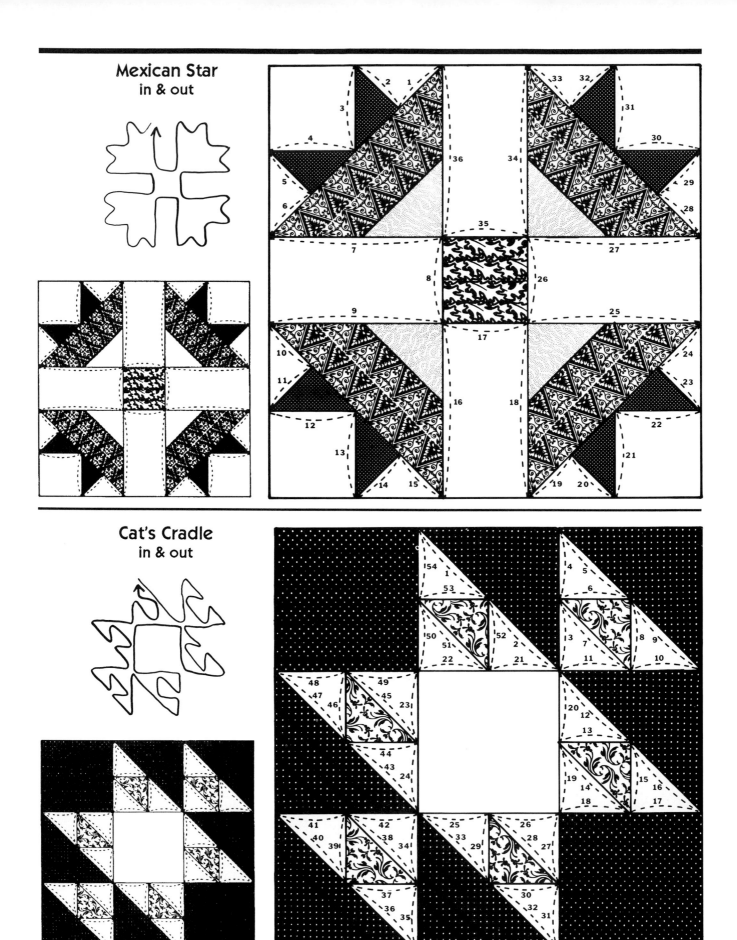

Mexican Star
in & out

Cat's Cradle
in & out

172 Barbara Johannah's Crystal Piecing

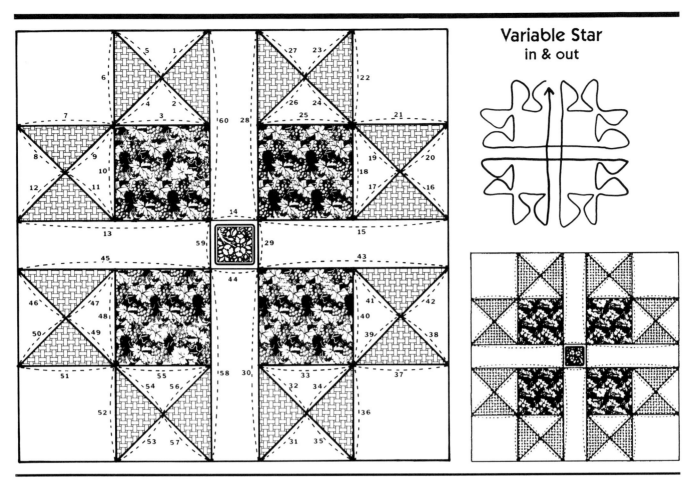

Variable Star
in & out

Tumbling Diamonds
spiral

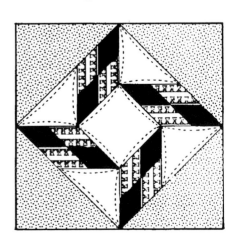

Mystery
spiral

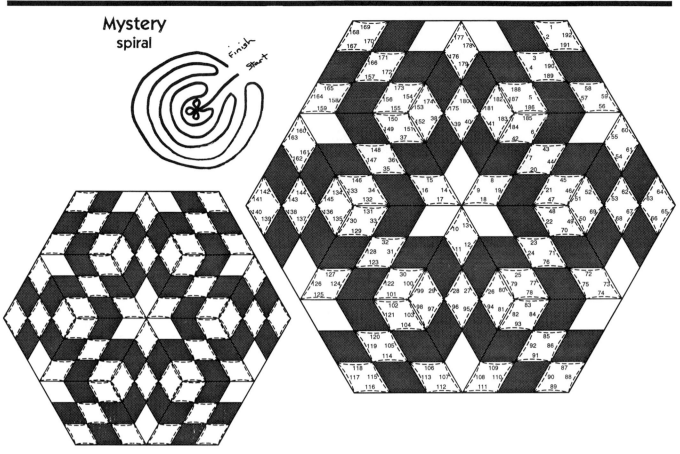

Medallion
spiral

I hope that once you grasp the principle of Continuous Curve Quilting, you will begin experimenting. Some ideas are better worked with the presser foot on; some, with free-machine quilting. Here are some ideas:

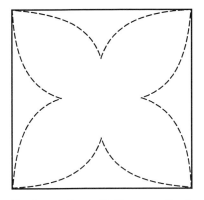

Continuous Curve Quilting goes floral

Continuous Curve Quilting goes straight

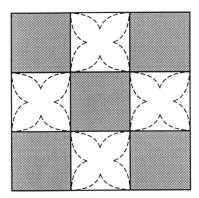

Floral Continuous Curve Quilting

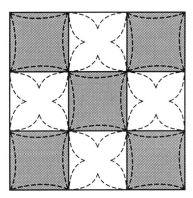

Floral plus basic Continuous Curve Quilting

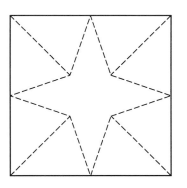

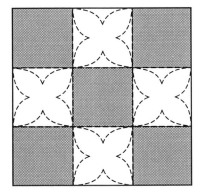

Floral Continuous Curve Quilting plus Stitch-in-the-Ditch

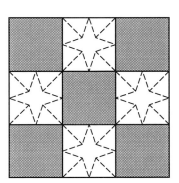

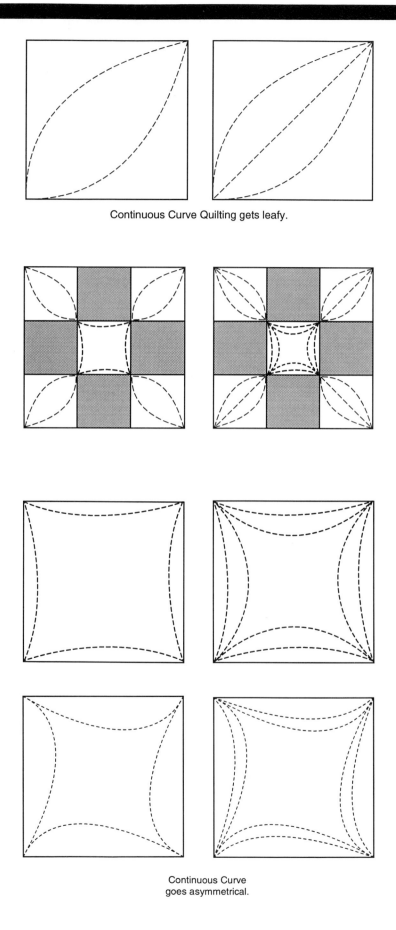

Continuous Curve Quilting gets leafy.

Continuous Curve
goes asymmetrical.

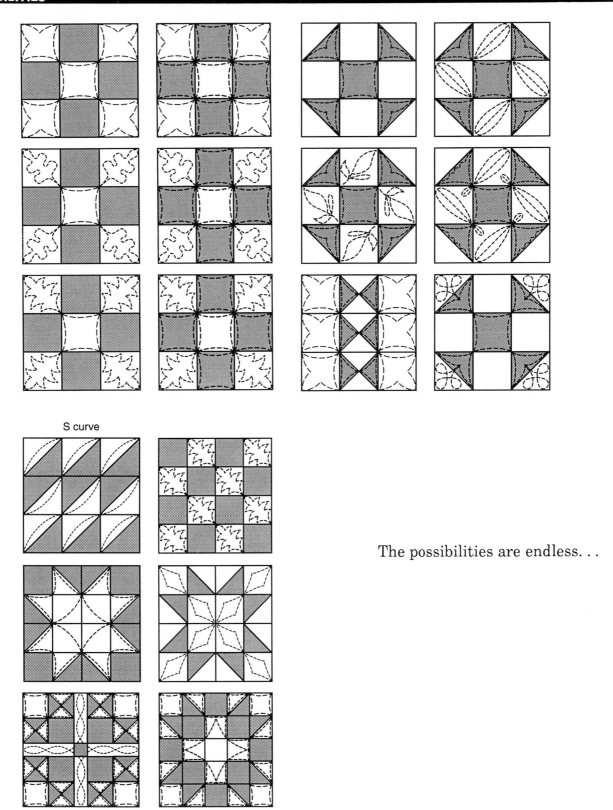

S curve

The possibilities are endless. . .

12.

How to Machine Quilt

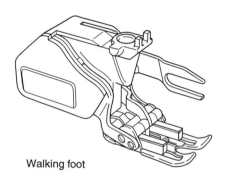

Walking foot

Darning foot

Materials and Tools

Now that you've explored ways to machine quilt, let's talk about how to do it.

Sewing Machine

Adjust your sewing machine so that it sews a good seam—clean out the bobbin area (including under the feed dogs), oil if appropriate, use a new 80(12) needle and good quality thread.

Sewing Machine Feet

A regular straight-stitch foot is adequate for Stitch-in-the-Ditch and Ernest Haight's Machine-Quilting Method, but a walking foot is better. For free-motion quilting such as Continuous Curve Quilting, a darning foot is desirable.

Throat Plate

Use a straight-stitch throat plate if you have one. It has a small hole and consequently the fabric can't be pulled into the hole.

Thread

Match the fiber content of your thread to your fabric. Use cotton thread on cotton fabric. If you don't want the thread to show, try a high-quality monofilament nylon thread for the top thread as Harriet Hargrave does. Experiment on scraps to balance the upper and lower threads.

Safety Pins

Ordinarily a quilt is thread-basted in order to keep the layers from shifting while quilting. This is often not adequate for quilting on the sewing machine. The sewing machine often distorts the piece in spite of the basting. Safety pins should be used liberally for basting, depending on the scale of your pattern pieces. Use at least one pin per pieced square and space them no more than 3" apart. The more thoroughly you pin, the less likely you are to have surprises on the back.

Batts

These are now available in a truly staggering variety of fibers and features. They vary in cost, ease of use, fiber content, thickness, degree of warmth, maximum quilting distance, and potential for bearding. Generally, use a thinner batt for machine quilting as it creates more definition than hand quilting.

My choices are simplified by the fact that I am sensitive to so many things. Polyester batts literally make me sick. When polyester touches my skin, it feels as though it's bearding through my skin—unpleasant.

Batt Choices

Here are some of your choices: 100% cotton, needlepunched "natural" cotton, 80% cotton/20% polyester, wool low to regular loft, silk, polyester low to regular loft, needlepunched polyester. (Choices based on batting chart in *Quilter's Newsletter Magazine* issue 241, adapted with permission.)

Quilting Line Markers

If you choose to mark your quilting lines, you will need a marker that produces a line that washes out easily. Test your quilt line marker on scrap fabric and wash it before using the marker on your quilt top. There are many to choose from and more always seem to be coming on the market.

Some quilters use masking tape for long straight lines. With enough practice many quilting lines don't need to be marked.

Preparing the Quilt Top

I use two ways, depending on the size of the quilt.

Envelope Method

Try this on Checkerboard (page 170), Medallion (page 174), Rail Fence (page 100) and smaller quilts.

1. Piece the backing so it is the same size as the quilt top.

Like most machine quilters, I safety-pin-baste my quilts with #0 or #1 brass safety pins. I secure the layers at a minimum of 2" intervals. Pinning frequently is an absolute necessity, but admittedly tedious. Using low-loft batting and all this pinning, I find no reason whatsoever to quilt from the center of the piece out. With the volume of pins I use, there is no shifting. I begin quilting from the outside edge into the center, rolling out of my way the quilted areas. The completed section rolls out quite flat, without the need of bicycle clips.

Once half the quilt is completed, I rotate the quilt to the opposite side and repeat the process.

Order of operation is important. Quilt the background filler first, stabilizing the layers, and finish with any free-motion patterns. This minimizes shift and provides a better layered surface for manipulation.

Linda Denner, author
Baby Quilts
Garden City, NY

I've been experimenting with a medium gray thread for machine quilting that crosses many colors and like the look.

3. Place batting on top of the quilt top. Cut batting 1/8" to 1/4" smaller than finished size.

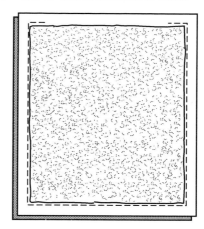

4. Roll up all the layers toward the open end. Do not smooth out as you roll.

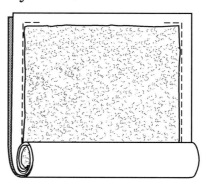

5. Open the end over the roll. Turn inside-out as you unroll.

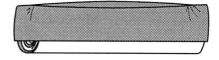

6. Tie or pin every 3", in preparation for quilting.

7. Blindstitch the open end.

Traditional Method

I always think of this as kitchen floor cleaning time. It's the only hard surface I have that's large enough. Unfold your batt ahead of time to relax the folds in it. The day before will do. Press your quilt top and quilt backing. Layer the backing rightside down, add the batt, and put the quilt rightside up on top. Each layer must be smooth and free of wrinkles. While you can do this by yourself, it is much easier to do with the help of others. When you've got it flat, start safety-pinning the three layers together. Pin about every 3". Make sure you pin between your quilting lines and not on them.

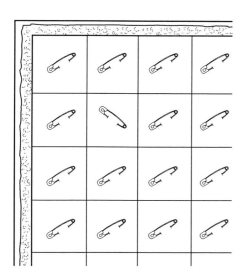

Layer backing, batting, and filling and pin every 3".

Machine Quilting

Roll up the side of the quilt that will be under the arm of the sewing machine. Some quilters use bicycle clips to keep it rolled as they sew. Have a large support area around your sewing machine so that the weight of the quilt does not pull on the sewing machine needle.

Move your quilt under the sewing machine foot to the place you wish to start quilting. Set the stitch length on zero and stitch in place to secure your beginning threads. Quilt your quilt, rerolling the portion under the machine as needed. Finish off your threads by again sewing in place.

The quality of your quilting depends upon your skill at machine quilting. Your level of skill depends upon how much you've practiced. With machine piecing, a mistake can be ripped out; a mistake in machine quilting is not so simply corrected. Like the little bird leaving the nest for the first time, you have one chance to machine quilt without foul-up. So prepare as much as possible. Practice machine quilting on plain fabric mini-quilts before trying it on a pieced quilt top. Using a patterned backing will hide any puckers. Also, before quilting your pieced top, quilt a small practice piece using the same batting to make sure your machine is correctly adjusted.

Tip My editor, Robbie Fanning, who is co-author of *The Complete Book of Machine Quilting*, likes to use a narrow zigzag (width 1, length 1.5) to machine quilt. It gives a softer look to the machine-quilting line.

Tip What if you will be quilting over both dark and light fabrics and don't want your stitching to show? See if your sewing machine can accommodate a cotton thread in the bobbin and a fine monofilament nylon top thread. That's what Harriet Hargrave uses.

Advantages of Machine Quilting

1. Speed! Blocks can be quilted in five or ten minutes. You will actually get those quilt tops quilted.

2. Three-dimensional beauty of quilting.

3. High relief/thin batt. Since machine quilting produces a higher relief than hand quilting, you can get the same effect with a thinner batt.

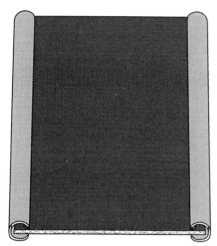

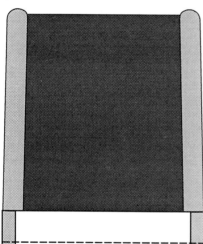

Binding

There are many methods to bind a quilt, but to keep things simple, I've used only two: turning the front border to the back or the backing to the front in a self-binding and applying a double-fold binding to the edge.

The double-fold binding can be either straight-grain or bias. Cut the binding 2" – 3" wide. Fold it in half, wrong sides together, and press. Stitch the cut edges to the sides of the quilt. Fold the edge over to the back and secure with a hand blind stitch.

Then cut strips slightly longer than the width of the quilt. Fold in half as before and press. Fold in one short end, align with one unfinished end of the quilt, and stitch. As you approach the other end, fold it in even with the quilt. Finish the seam. Turn the binding to the back and hand stitch.

Rather than having to piece binding strips, it is easier to make continuous bias.

1. Cut a square of cloth in half diagonally.

2. Join the two pieces to form a parallelogram by connecting the two "with grain" sides. Use a 1/4" seam and press open.

3. Mark lines 2" – 3" apart, parallel to the edges.

4. Seam the parallelogram together to form a tube, moving the first line over one place and matching all other lines. Cut along the continous line.

I learned this method from the Santa Clara Valley Quilt Assocation.

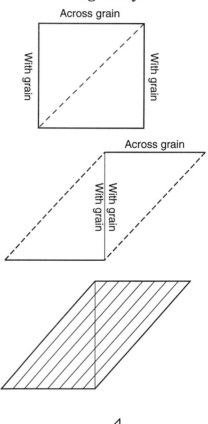

Barbara Johannah's Crystal Piecing

Part Five:

Design Your Own Quilt

Planning a quilt may be as simple as knowing you want to reproduce a specific quilt—or it may involve longer hours designing, testing, sewing, and quilting an original design.

This part of the book examines 1) how to design your own original blocks; 2) how to analyze any block and adapt its piecing to Quick Quiltmaking methods; and 3) how to calculate yardage for either.

13.

Designing Half-Square Triangle Quilts

11   91

If you're ready to go beyond traditional patterns, try creating your own. It's fun and simple to do.

This chapter shows you the methods and tools for manipulating any design element to make a block, then how to play with blocks to make quilts. Remember, the simpler the design fragment you start with, the more potential it has. If working with one shape, explore all of the ways it can be manipulated—repeat it on a grid, rotate it, reflect it, or combine it with another pattern or with several manipulation methods.

At this point you are merely generating designs, unconcerned about how to piece them. Later we'll look at ways to execute a design.

Although you can use these methods with any pattern or shape, a good place to start is with a Half-Square Triangle and Jane Warnick's Element Key.

A Half-Square Triangle can be placed on the page in only four positions:

If you combine two of these positions, you can arrange them in only 16 ways:

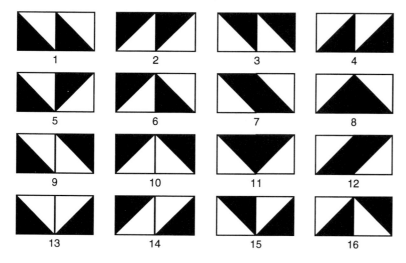

If you combine three of these positions, you can arrange them in 64 ways. But if you combine all four positions, you have 256 possible combinations. The combinations could be shown in a straight line of four Half-Square Triangles each, but they are more useful to us stacked two on two.

In the Half-Square Triangle Key on pages 186 and 187, Jane Warnick has arbitrarily numbered the combinations from 1 to 256. This is handy in two ways.

First, you will be able to keep track of which elements you use to generate quilt patterns.

Secondly, you can take an important date in someone's life, such as a birthday, and present the person with a unique block or quilt. For example, if your important day is June 23, 1951, you might select elements 6, 23, 19, and 51 and design a block or quilt with the techniques in this chapter.

Choosing a significant date is just a way to kick you out of thinking in a rut. It's a take-off point for designing. I have found, however, that selecting just two elements rather than all four yields more viable patterns with fewer operations.

The Half-Square Triangle Element Key on pages 186 and 187 is an incredible aid to designing with Half-Square Triangles developed by Jane Warnick of Houston, TX. She based it on the design exploration work of a 17th century monk, Dominique Douat. He worked with ceramic tiles, placing the tiles four in a row. Jane reworked the system as it appears in the Key so it would be more usable for quilters.

6   23   19   51

6 and 23

Use mirrors to reflect (page 191).

Half-Square Triangle Element Key

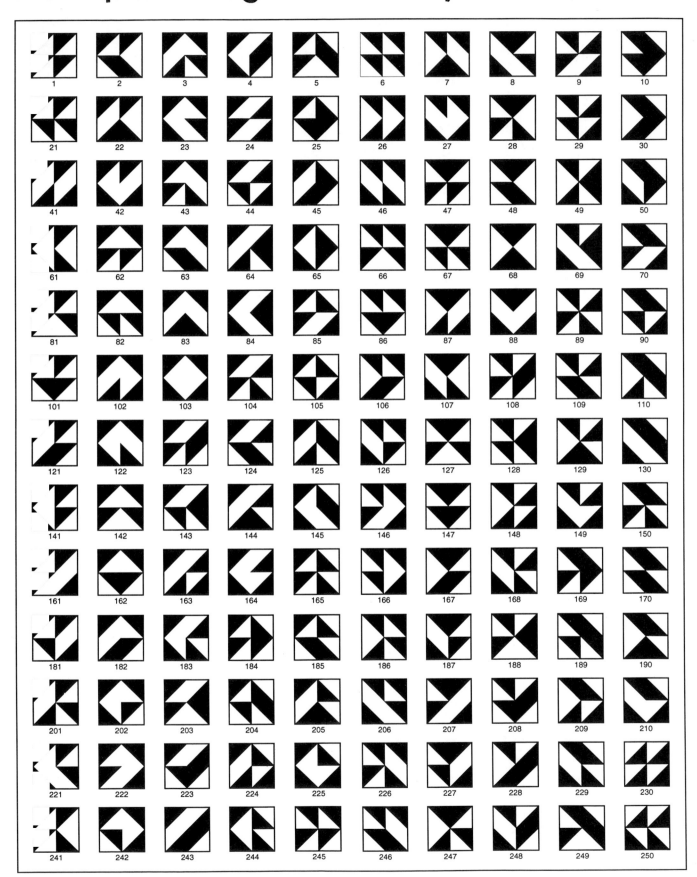

Lyn Piercy, *Raspberry Sherbet*, 88" x 101"

Carlene Chang, *Nikki's Quilt*

Jean Ray Laury, *Diamond Star*

Doris Hoover, *Lightning T's*, 85½" square

Carla Rodio, *Appalachian Trails #2*, 60" square

Janet Hartnell-Williams, *Triangles #2*, 55" square

Jean Ray Laury, *Stars & Stripes in Brown*, 51" square

Beryl Self, *Flowers & Baskets*, 53" square

Mary Whitehead, *Pacific Flyway,* 60" x 78"

Collection of Pilgrim-Roy Antiques, *Devil's Puzzle Variation,* 78" x 84"

Joan Schulze, *Oahu*, 72" square; © 1981
Schulze; collection of R. Dakin, International

Linda Denner, *Call Me Ishmael*, 39" x 33"

Linda Lillard, *Aurora, the Dawn*, 61" square

Sarah Beth Tennison, *Bird Quilt*, 75" x 94"

Jennifer Amor, *Quick Patch Star Sampler*, 89" x 104"

Half-Square Triangle Element Key

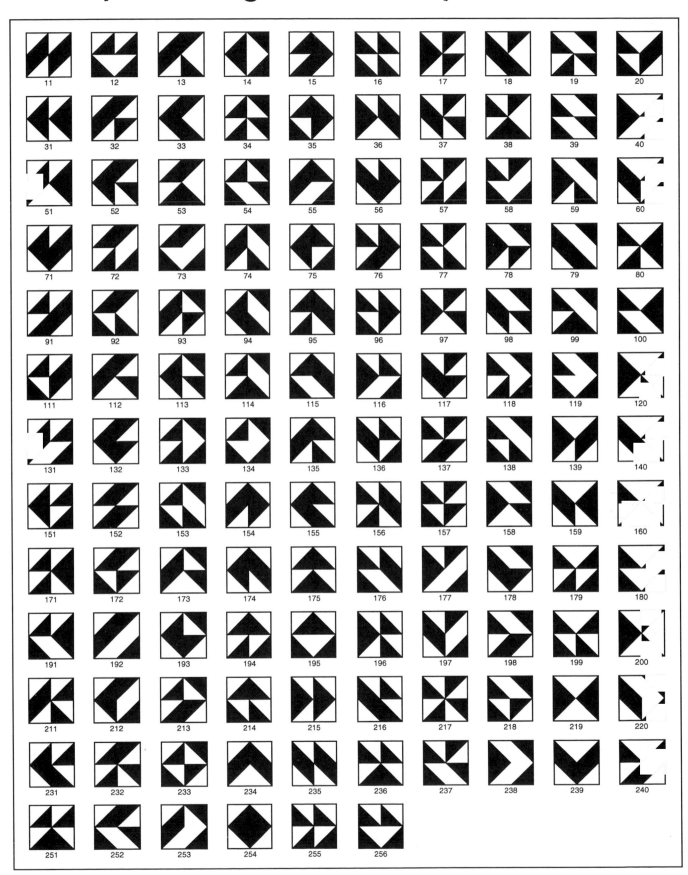

Jane Warnick prefers to use the word "translation" for "repetition."

Block Formation

Let's take various design elements from the Element Key and explore three methods for manipulating an element to build a new quilt block: repetition, rotation, and reflection. Then we'll explore manipulating blocks to make a quilt.

Repetition

Repetition is, obviously, repeating a design element along an established network. Three networks apply to quilting: Square, Half-Drop, and Brick.

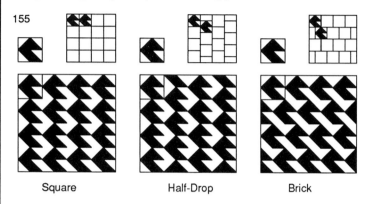

| Square | Half-Drop | Brick |

You try it with one design element. Pick any number and try it on a grid.

You can use a rectangular grid if you first generate a rectangular block. Draw or stamp your element (see page X), then rotate it 180° (turning it upside down) and place it under the original element.

121

Repeating these rectangles on the rectangular grid generates a striped pattern. If you place them on a staggered network (not technically a full half-drop grid), you will have a pattern with a strong diagonal bent.

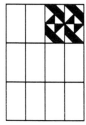

110

Rectangular grid

Staggered element on rectangular grid

Chapter 13. **Design Half Squares** | **189**

> *"* Barbara was one of the first to devise creative, logical ways to speed up quiltmaking in the early days of the current enthusiastic revival. Her ideas are even more useful today, fifteen years later, since quilting mentality has matured.
>
> Her Continuous Curve method of machine quilting is so current since many us are switching from hand labor to machine quilting, which is finally gaining more and more acceptance from quilt critics.
>
> It is wonderful to study Barbara's compiled combinations of half-square triangles. I love it when somebody else has figured out endless combinations of designs so all I have to do is scan the possibilities and visualize the options in my own color favorites. *"*

Charlotte Patera, fabric artist
Grass Valley, CA

Rotation

Rotation is turning the design element one-quarter at a time through a square. You designate one corner of the design element as point A and place this point at the center of a square equal to the size of four design elements. Each design can be rotated around any of its four corners.

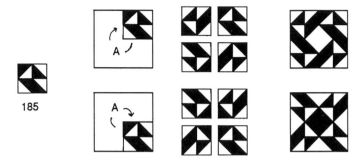

You may also rotate a design around a center square, using either a light or dark square in the center. Rotate the design element 90° for each neighboring position, either clockwise or counter-clockwise.

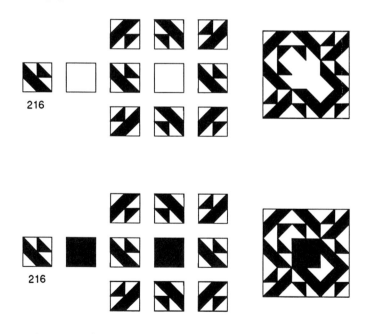

Alternately, combine two elements into a rectangle and rotate the rectangle around a center square.

If you are working with graph paper and a pen (see page 201), you will need to draw your element on a separate paper so you can physically turn it. It is very difficult to visualize the position of the element in its four orientations. Mark the corner you are rotating around with a small circle.

Draw a circle or mark at the pivot point so you don't get confused.

Reflection

Reflection is the result of copying what you see when you hold mirrors against your original design element. The easiest way to see these patterns is to place mirrors on two adjacent sides of your design element (a 90° angle) or through the middle at a 45° angle and look at the patterns at the point where the mirrors meet.

The mirrors should be no-frame and about 3" x 4". I've seen some in craft stores that are not glass mirrors but that work perfectly well. Hinge the back with a piece of tape (or buy them from some quilt stores already hinged).

Holding the mirrors at a 90 degree angle to each other. The mirrors meet at point B in this example.

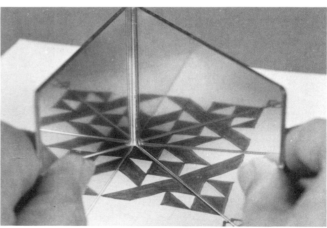

Examples when a different point is used at the center.

Chapter 13. **Design Half Squares** **191**

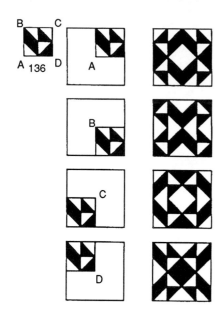

Examples when a different point is used at the center.

When you use the mirrors one-by-one on your design elements, you will quickly see many different patterns. This is a fast weeding-out process in which you need only record those patterns you like. You will re-discover many of your old favorite traditional blocks, along with an infinite number of new ones which are in the traditional mode. These are the most restful patterns within the system. The more symmetry you have, the more balance and repose.

Step 1: Combine two elements into one pattern, repeating each across the square from each other.

Step 2: Place the mirrors at the angles indicated. Look at the new pattern. If you like it, draw it on graph paper.

This combination of design elements can yield eight views. Here are two:

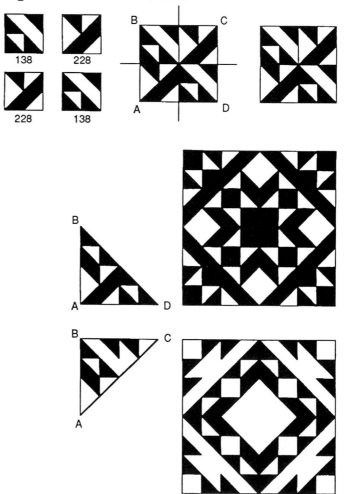

Use two mirrors to find the other six patterns that lie within this combination. Look at BCA, ACD, CDB, DAC, and CAB.

Nine-Patch Manipulations

To make life simple for you, the above manipulations were done on a four-patch block, but you can apply the same maneuvers to any other underlying block grid, such as nine-patch. Naturally this gives you a larger, more complex block than does starting with a four-patch.

Rotation around a central point

Here are a few 36-patch designs.

✏️ If you still have a Rubik's Cube around, a toy from many years ago, you can easily explore nine-patch design. Peel off the colored plastic squares and cut them in half along the diagonal. Return one half to each square in the same orientation. Now you can manipulate the cube to make nine-patch designs. When you find one you like, record it on graph paper or carve a stamp (see page 202).

✏️ A quilter once wanted me to figure out the number of possibilities for nine-patch variations. I just laughed. It's an enormous number.

Block Manipulation

Once you have established a block pattern which you like, try it in combination with another block, either traditional or one you have discovered. Here we are setting the blocks side-by-side.

Another possibility is to reverse the dark/light coloring of the block you have chosen and combine with your original block. (The number of the reverse block can also be found in the Half-Square Triangle Element Key on pages 186 – 187.)

The traditional pattern Devil's Puzzle is an example of alternating your original block and the reverse coloring of your original block.

Try combining your pattern with a simple nine-patch block. These are on a square grid, alternating the patterns on each row and each column.

Overlapping blocks can form interesting new patterns. This would be much easier to design on a computer (see page 199).

The possibilities for original design are vast. Try changing the shape of your block by stretching squares, moving the center off-center (see Log Cabin ideas on page 111), or blurring seam lines by combining piecing with appliqué.

I've left the top row of blocks in each pattern complete, to help you see the origin of the pattern.

Cupid's Arrow

overlap block 1/2 in one direction

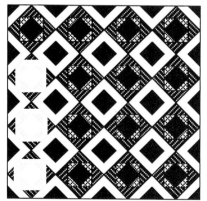

continuous setting, no overlapping

overlap block 1/4 in one direction

overlap block 3/4 in one direction

overlap block 1/4 in both directions

Borders

You can use the same methods you used to explore pattern design to generate border patterns. Try one of these six ways.

1. Repeat: Repeat along the strip.

227

2. Rotate: Turn the element 180°, then repeat it.

227

Rotate   Repeat

3. Mirror reflect/bottom: Hold the mirror on the *bottom* of the element to form a rectangle. Then repeat it.

227

Repeat

4. Mirror reflect/side: Hold the mirror on the *right side* of the element to form a rectangle. Then repeat it.

227

Repeat

5. Mirror glide: Hold a mirror on the bottom of the element as in #4 and move the resultant mirror image beside the original element to form a rectangle. Then repeat it.

227

Repeat

114

Chapter 13. **Design Half Squares**   **197**

6. Mirror reflect/bottom and side: Hold mirrors on both the *bottom and one side* of the element. First do #3. Reflect the entire rectangle to make the right side of the square. Then repeat it. At the corners, I used a mirror at 45° until I found a pattern I liked.

227

Repeat

Tools for Generating Designs

There are so many ways to generate design. All are fun to do. Of course, each has its strengths. I've divided them into high tech/high cost and low tech/low cost. What I'm talking about here is money. At the high-tech end we have the computer and its printer and at the low-cost end we have an assortment of familiar items, including graph paper, pencils, erasers, craft knives, copy machines, and mirrors. (Copy machines are in the low-cost group because you're buying copies, not the machine.)

It isn't so much a question of what each of these items can do, but what they do well, efficiently, and at a reasonable cost. I use all of these methods for gener-

Each method of design manipulation and recording influences in subtle ways the design that you create. The computer is quite common now for creating finished art work, but not yet commonly used by quilters as a design tool. As it becomes cheaper and more widely used, I look forward to seeing how it changes the quilts that quilters create.

ating design. I offer my experience with them as a starting point. So much depends on personal preferences and styles of working that each quilter, through experimentation, should find what works best for her or him.

Methods of Approach

The four methods I use most are computers, graph paper, copy machines, and carved stamp. (I used to design with the toy called Rubik's Cube, but it is no longer manufactured.) You may find a better method that works for you. Do it—and write me about your methods.

1. Computers

Computers vary tremendously in their cost. In general, computers offer faster and more precisely drawn results.

What the computer can do

The computer provides the power. In general, the more money you spend, the more powerful the computer you can buy. A more powerful computer works faster. (With my first computer, I used to read a book while it was working.) Writing takes very little computer power. Most any computer can write satisfactorily. Drawing takes a much more powerful computer to do anything of consequence. Speed is important in a computer. It takes a lot of computer power to process your drawing commands. The level of power of your computer sets the upper limits of what you can do on your computer.

The programs you use with your computer determine what you can do on your computer. I think of it this way: the computer has the I.Q. and the program has the education. I do most of my work with the MacDraw program on a Macintosh computer. (There are similar programs for other brands of computers.) This program's strength is squares and half-square triangles and most any pattern composed of 90° and 45° angles. Most easily learned computer drawing programs work with squares and half-square triangles. You can do repetition, rotation, and reflection almost as fast as you can think.

This is a major advantage of drawing on a computer. With a pencil on paper I often lose my train of thought. I can think up "what if's" so much faster than I can sketch them. While the computer isn't as fast as your thinking, its increased speed helps you get down your ideas before you forget them.

Check out the programs and computers that are available to make sure that they are compatible.

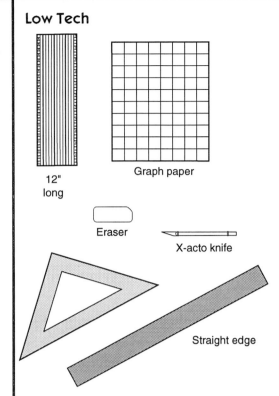

Low Tech

12" long

Graph paper

Eraser

X-acto knife

Straight edge

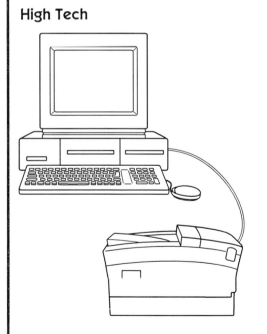

High Tech

Using a computer

When you draw geometric shapes with a drawing program, all of your lines are straight, not curved.

You draw the outline of the shape you want and "fill" it with a selected background pattern.

Patterns are formed by alternately duplicating, then positioning your design fragment.

Duplicating is accomplished by the press of a button. Mistakes can be corrected with a push of the button. Once you have the drawing the way you want it, copy it with a push of the button, and play with the copy, trying out changes on the copy. It really is all accomplished with a push of the mouse button. It's fun, too.

There isn't anything, however, you can do on the computer that you can't do with a pencil, paper, and time.

248   Duplicate

    (approx)

Rotate left   Rotate right   Flip vertical   Flip horizontal

Background patterns can be added.

Repetition is achieved by alternately duplicating and positioning the element.

To make a rotation pattern, alternately duplicate, rotate, and position.

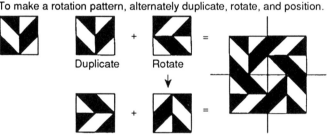

Duplicate   Rotate

To make a reflected pattern, alternately duplicate, flip vertical or horizontal, and position.

   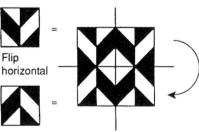

Duplicate   Flip horizontal

Reflect top element

2. Graph paper

In addition to graph paper in squares, you can buy equilateral triangle graph paper and many specialty graph papers at art stores and engineering supply stores. When selecting square graph paper, four, five, or six squares to the inch is recommended, as any graph paper which is smaller (eight or more squares to the inch) is too hard on the eyes. Expresso, a bold-point pen by Sanford, works well in designing, as do Prismacolor colored pencils. Do small areas of design and then duplicate them on a copy machine (see #3 below). See pages 245 – 247 for 45°, diamond, and 60° grids for you to photocopy.

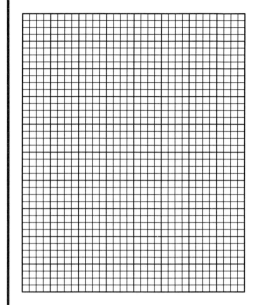

3. Copy machine

Copy machines are marvelous design tools. Use the processes of repetition, rotation, and reflection on the design elements from the Half-Square Triangle Element Key (pages 186 – 187) to design blocks. Then copy them many times. Keep copying, cutting up, rearranging, and re-copying to your heart's content.

Fill a page of graph paper with your design ideas, blocks, or other design fragments. Make 10 or so copies on a copy machine. Cut out the blocks, manipulate, and paste them down when you have discovered a pattern you wish to record.

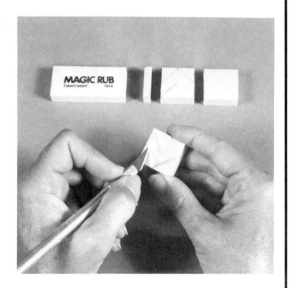

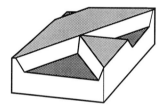

Stamping another stamp.

4. Carved stamp

If instant gratification appeals to you, then definitely try carving a rubber stamp from an eraser and stamping the patterns. You may use several different kinds of erasers, all under $1 a piece. The plastic erasers by Farber Castell are the easiest to carve. They are long-lasting and will also give a good stamping. The art gum eraser is the cheapest. It is also the most difficult to carve because it crumbles. The pink pearl eraser is also difficult to carve, not because it crumbles, but because it is made of a tougher material. It will, however, last a long time and stamp well.

The plastic erasers come in several sizes, but for the most economical use, the 1" x 2-1/4" is recommended. You cut the eraser into two 1" squares, draw graph lines on the eraser, color in the part to remain and begin carving. The remaining parts will print dark. You will need a craft knife (X-acto is inexpensive and good), paper, and a stamp pad. All of these supplies are available in art, office-supply, and large drug stores.

You should then be able to lift out the part you wish to remove by putting the point of the knife under these cuts and wiggling it around. This will yield a stamp which is the mirror image of the element you selected (you will use this stamp in the exploration process).

Now stamp this stamp on the other 1"-square eraser and carve as before, removing the *uncolored* sections. Voilà! You now have a stamp of the original element and a stamp of its mirror image. Depending on the element chosen, you now have two stamps which may represent from 1 to 8 different numbers on the key.

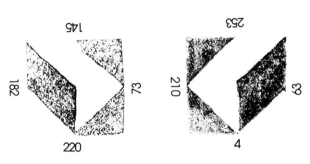

This method uses the eraser as it is or mounts it with rubber cement on the bottom of an inexpensive plastic box from a dime store. These boxes come in various sizes from 1" to 4" square. You may also mount four stamps on a 2" square box and stamp a page in minutes. Jane once stamped an entire 11" x 14" sketchbook in one evening with only two such stamps.

This method has other advantages beside speed. The stamping is generally a value of gray, and you can add other values of color without redrawing the design. It also reproduces well on copy machines if you want to try different colorways. Finally you can use a textile paint or dye to stamp the pattern on cloth and create your own fabric or miniature quilt.

I recently taught elementary-school math teachers using stamps. We used Dr. Scholl's insoles cut into Half-Square Triangles and glued with white glue to the end of 1" x 1" wood blocks. The teachers glued the mirror image of the element onto the opposite end of the block. Then they could easily switch from one to the other for stamping.

If you want to do this:	High Tech/High Cost Way
90° and 45° angles	Computer and printer
squares, rectangles, Half-Square and Quarter-Square Triangles and other similar shapes	Most common and most less-expensive drawing programs can do these.
true 45° diamonds, equilateral triangles, 60° diamonds, hexagons and other shapes based on a 60° angle	This takes a powerful program such as Illustrator. Expensive and hard to learn, but it can do anything, including 90° and 45° angles, shapes, and everything in between. A powerful computer is required to run this program. Except for illustrations for publications or some such high-end use, stick with equilateral-triangle graph paper.
repetition	The two commands for repetition on the computer are duplication and position. The computer shows its speed when repeating larger sections of a design.
rotation	Computer commands: duplicate, rotate, and position. Again the computer shows its speed when repeating larger sections of a design.
reflection	Commands: duplicate, flip vertical or horizontal, and position. MacDraw and other basic drawing programs reflect on the vertical and horizontal axis, but not on the diagonal. You can get around this by redrawing small portions, erasing, redrawing small portions along the diagonal axis and then copying, reflecting, rotating, and positioning. The computer is faster for recording reflected patterns.
camera-ready copy	Varies with the computer and programs. At the high end you can do good versatile work at high speed. If you're paying to have a job done, or are being paid, it's cheaper to do it on a computer due to the shorter time it takes to do camera-ready work.
overlapping	The computer shines here. This is play and the results are serendipity. You have no idea what you're going to come up with.
copying large chunks of designs and then changing them	I think of this as "slice and dice." It's fun and fast. Being able to change designs quickly changes the final design. The computer is fast at copying large designs. You can play What-If? easily, but one design at a time. Working with a computer is like looking through binoculars. It's all three, but you can only see part of it at one time. Beware: Complex designs that take minutes to draw can takes hours to print out.
progression of pattern formation	When you bring a drawing back on the screen that you have worked on previously, it doesn't appear all at once. It comes on piece-by-piece in the order you drew it. Seeing the progression of pattern formation gives you additional ideas for designs.

If you want to do this:	Low Tech/Low Cost Way
90° and 45° angles, squares, rectangles, Half-Square and Quarter-Square Triangles and other similar shapes	Square graph paper, and pencils, rubber stamps made from erasers, copy machine
true 45° diamonds, equilateral triangles, 60° diamonds, hexagons and other shapes based on a 60° angle	Equilateral-triangle graph paper and pencils, copy machine
repetition	Rubber stamping is faster than the computer for doing smaller design components such as elements from the Half-Square Triangle Element Key.
rotation	Rubber stamping is faster than the computer for doing smaller design components such as elements from the Half-Square Triangle Element Key.
reflection	Mirrors with pencil and paper. This is the most personally satisfying way to do reflection. Also the most versatile. You can hold the mirrors at any angle and look at various formations in rapid succession. Using mirrors is faster at pattern formation, but slower at recording patterns. Wonderful for exploring ways of turning a corner on borders.
camera-ready copy	The choices range from freehand drawings to T-square, ink pens, and press-on backgrounds.
overlapping	Tracing paper or acetate. Possible, but tedious.
copying large chunks of designs and then changing them	Copy machine. Pencil sketch blocks or other chunks of designs. Fill the page. Make 5-10 copies. Cut apart and tape back together. Copy again. I do this even though I have a computer. You can spread out all your designs over the whole table and refer back and forth easily.
progression of pattern formation	Same as copying large chunks of designs (above).

Playing "What-If?"

I like to play, watching where the shapes will lead me. My best efforts don't come from sitting before the blank paper or computer screen and trying to draw something pleasing. Trying to do a final drawing the first time I sit down, I either end up drawing the same traditional pattern over and over or I'm just stalled. For me, the best approach is to see where the design leads me, to take a design fragment and play What-If?

1. Dancing Brackets

This one I did on the computer. I started with 192 and 233 from The Half-Square Triangle Element Key. I like to choose one element with some internal symmetry, using it for the outer corners of the block, and one element with a strong diagonal for the middle of the side. This gives me a block with both symmetry and movement. It's a nice starting point.

First I combined them into a rectangle. Then I rotated them around a center square. I then reflected this block pattern, holding the mirrors along the side and bottom, and took a look. Did I like what I saw?

192

233

Barbara Johannah's Crystal Piecing

Yes, I liked the pattern, so I tried repeating it four times in a square. Then I extended the four sides so I would have full patterns.

Did anything suggest itself? I saw brackets which I liked. I emphasized them.

I like all the movement the brackets made, but when all the movement and the Op Art quality started to make my eyes dance, I took out most of the brackets. (Perhaps with variations in light and dark and color you can take this pattern further.)

What could I simplify? What could I combine?
Result: a simple, calm, traditional pattern enlivened
with Dancing Brackets.

Try Dancing Brackets on other traditional patterns, like Audrey's Choice and Brown Goose.

I prefer the first two, because they are simpler
patterns. In the second two, I don't care for the center
tip of the bracket touching the blocks. What do you
think?

2. Intertwining Cables

Playing What-If? again, I wanted to see what would happen if I put all of the brackets facing sideways, not horizontally and vertically. Result: Intertwining Cables instead of Dancing Brackets.

Next I wondered what the result would be if the brackets went in both directions, horizontally and vertically, on the perimeter of the quilt.

3. Op-Art Reflection

A completely different look is achieved by repeat-edly reflecting portions of the original reflected block. This would be much easier to execute on a computer.

4. Interwoven Philos

This pattern is formed by first rotating the design element around a central point. Then I created a second block with the reverse coloring of the original block. Now I simply repeated each block horizontally in alternate rows.

Once I had the basic quilt, I began to play with various areas, adding pattern and value, changing some shapes. Here's the result.

This gives you an idea of how I play with designs. There were others which showed less promise than these; some, so awful they went straight into the scrap paper pile without a moment's hesitation. Others I pondered awhile to see if there were any possibilities hidden within.

Blocks Don't Have to be Square!

This pattern is formed with the rotation of four unusually shaped blocks.

In the previous chapter, we explored generating your own block and quilt designs. But you may see a block, traditional or otherwise, that you'd like to quick-piece. In this chapter I'll show you how to analyze any block.

Be aware that how you break down a quilt pattern for machine-piecing methods is often different from how you would break the same pattern down if you were cutting out pieces one by one. Look for the bones of the pattern. Forget color and the patterns printed on the fabric. Look at the quilt in black and white. Look only at the lines of the pattern, the lines that you see, and most importantly, the underlying structural lines.

I don't follow set rules for figuring out how to machine piece patterns. I "see" the pattern on a grid and I "see" how the pattern should be done. This will be easier for people who are more spatially than verbally inclined, but I think most quilters can do it if they practice. This is easier to do if you stop thinking in words.

Some attributes flag a pattern as one that can be pieced using Quick-Quiltmaking methods. Look for:

1. An underlying grid

2. Sequence of color repeats in same shape

3. Mirror-image shapes

4. Straight-seam sewing

5. If none of the above help, ask yourself, "Could any of these combinations of pieces fit on strata?"

To piece these shapes, see pages 23 – 80 on Crystal Piecing and pages 81 – 146 on Strips and Strata.

In the next pages, let's look at each of these attributes.

14.

How to Analyze Any Block

1. An Underlying Grid

Patterns that can be placed on an underlying grid can be made with quick machine-piecing methods. Find major vertical, horizontal, and/or diagonal seam lines that slice all the way through the pattern. Then find secondary lines. Place the quilt on one of the following three grids.

Square Grid

Put squares, rectangles, and right triangles on a square-grid graph paper. These shapes have 90° and 45° angles. Some stars are composed of Half-Square Triangles.

45° Diamond Grid

Put 45° diamonds on this grid for a true visual appearance. This grid is available from quilting supply sources. You can put true 8-pointed stars on a square grid for sketching, but be aware that your drawing will appear distorted. Piecing information on diamonds is on pages 113 – 119. See page 246 for a blank grid.

Equilateral Triangle Grid

Put 6-pointed stars, hexagons, and triangles with three equal sides on equilateral triangle grid graph paper, available at engineering supply or large stationery stores. These shapes must be formed on this graph paper. They can't be formed on square graph paper. Be sure to read pages 127 – 146 for piecing information on equilateral triangles. See page 247 for a blank 60° grid.

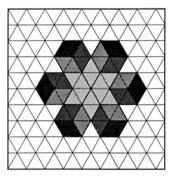

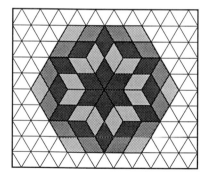

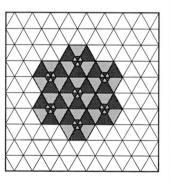

2. Sequence of Color Repeats in the Same Shape

Look for a row of squares, rectangles, or diamonds. Isolate the repeat. Then extend the lines of the repeat to make strips and strata. See page 82 for basic information on Strips and Strata.

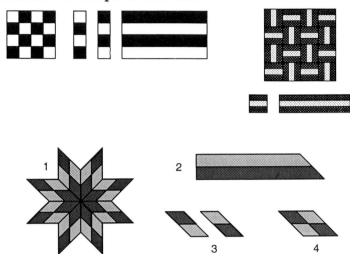

3. Mirror-Image Shapes

These are usually in pairs, but there may be multiples of more than two. Find the pairs by overlaying a grid on the block or quilt. Explode the pieces. Then identify the piecing method (e.g., Half-Square Triangles or strips and strata). See the chapters on Crystal Piecing starting on page 24 for piecing information.

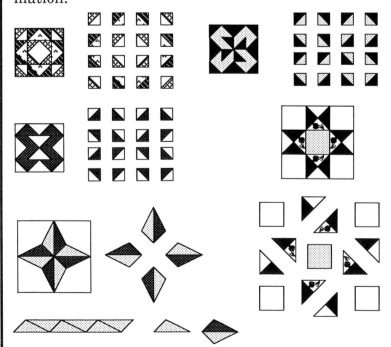

4. Straight-Seam Sewing

Find a straight line slicing along various shaped pieces. Isolate the repeat block. Explode the shape along the straight line. Then identify the resulting shape and how to piece it. For the examples below, see Equilateral Triangles on page 127 and Paired Quilts on page 139.

5. Hidden Strata

If none of the above help, ask yourself, could any of these combinations of pieces fit on strata? You may not be able to quick-piece all parts of a block, but some part may be eligible. The clue is repetition of a shape, no matter how odd to conventional thinking.

In a case such as on the right, you may be able to do some quick cutting, such as cutting long strips and slicing off the center squares, even though the rest of the pattern may not lend itself to quick quiltmaking.

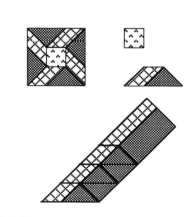

Practice in Analyzing Blocks

In the following examples I will analyze the pattern, determine the various ways in which this pattern could be constructed, and decide the best machine method of constructing the pattern, as well as whether it is a pattern that is better worked by cutting out individual pieces. Many patterns can be constructed in more than one way and many patterns are not worth doing with Quick Quiltmaking methods.

Remember seam allowances.

Example 1.

In this pattern, all lines are either vertical or horizontal. This pattern obviously fits on a square grid. You can draw four lines all the way through the pattern. This divides the pattern into five rows composed of squares and rectangles. The outside rows numbered 1 are the same. The rows numbered 2 are the same. One row is numbered 3. Each row is made with strips and strata. If the overall block finishes at 10", then each row finishes at 2". (Ten inches divided by 5 rows equals two inches.)

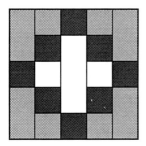

☑ An underlying grid

☑ Sequence of color repeats in same shape

❏ Mirror-image shapes

☑ Straight-seam sewing

❏ If none of the above help, ask yourself, "Could any of these combinations of pieces fit on a strata?"

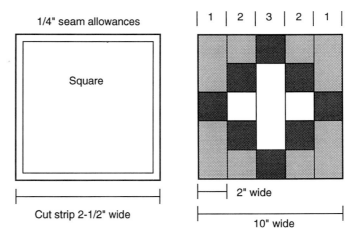

1/4" seam allowances

Square

Cut strip 2-1/2" wide

| 1 | 2 | 3 | 2 | 1 |

2" wide

10" wide

I will explain Row #2 first because it is the easiest to understand. Row #2 is composed of five 2" squares (finished size). Seam allowances must be added. Each strip you will need for this row must be cut:

2-1/2" wide to finish 2" (1/4" + 2" + 1/4" = 2-1/2").

Row #2

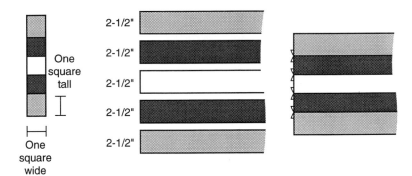

Row #1 is somewhat different. The center square is again cut from a 2-1/2" strip, but the adjoining pieces are, as you can see, rectangles, not squares. By studying and measuring the drawing you can see that each rectangle is one finished square wide by two finished squares long. But there is no need to piece squares to make the rectangle. Cut a rectangle with the measurement of two finished squares instead. Therefore, the width of the strip for cutting must be equal to two finished squares plus a seam allowance on each side. That makes a 4-1/2" strip (1/4" + 2" + 2" + 1/4").

Row #1

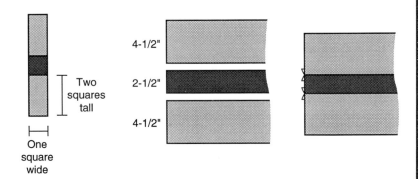

One day when my son was about four, his grandmother admonished him not to write in his book. His response was, "Momma writes in her books and she cuts them up, too."

If you own the book, draw in it, mentally converse with the author, tape additional information onto its pages, and even cut it up—it will aid your understanding. Do it!

In deciding on finished block sizes, measuring for cutting in whole inches is usually easiest. Rather than mark in fractions and finish in whole inches, mark in whole numbers and finish in fractions. For example, mark each strip 2" wide and finish the square 1-1/2".

Row #3 is unique. The outside squares are again cut from 2-1/2" strips. The proportions of the inner rectangle are one square by three squares. The width of the strip for cutting must then be equal to three finished squares plus seam allowance on each side. That is a 6-1/2" strip (1/4" + 6" + 1/4").

Row #3

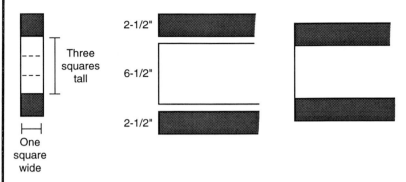

Also remember in calculating yardage that there are twice as many rows of Row #1 and Row #2 than of Row #3. Therefore, you will need twice as many strips to make twice as many panels to result in twice as many rows.

Example 2.

This next block is basically the same in construction as the last one. I won't go into the detail of the measurements because if you understand the last one, you will understand this one. The difference is in the border triangles. With blocks such as this one, it is easier to do the entire block with strips and trim to finish rather than fitting in precut triangles. You will "waste" fabric, but not your precious time in measuring and cutting small triangles and undoubtedly sewing the wrong side into the block.

☑ An underlying grid

☑ Sequence of color repeats in same shape

❏ Mirror-image shapes

☑ Straight-seam sewing

❏ If none of the above help, ask yourself, "Could any of these combinations of pieces fit on a strata?"

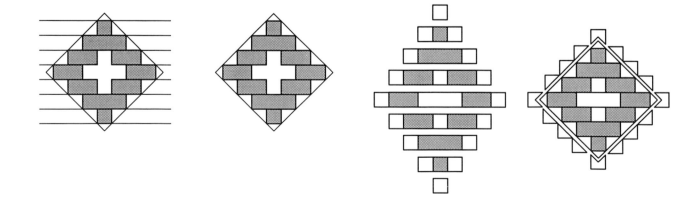

Example 3.

This pattern is an extension of the previous one. Look at the block. Do you see parallel lines? Do you see the same shape repeated in a sequence around the center block? Notice that the repeat block is composed of two different sequences of strips. That means this block can be constructed with strips and strata in two different sequences of strips.

☑ An underlying grid

☑ Sequence of color repeats in same shape

❑ Mirror-image shapes

☑ Straight-seam sewing

❑ If none of the above help, ask yourself, "Could any of these combinations of pieces fit on a strata?"

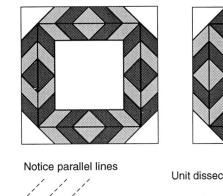

Notice parallel lines

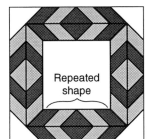

Unit dissected

Repeat unit

One unit mirror image

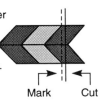

Turn sidewards for convenience.
Extend parallel lines.

Cut strips. Sew strata.

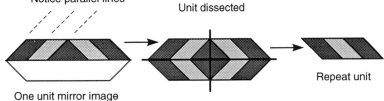

Slice half of strips at one 45-degree angle,
half at opposite angle.

Sew slices together in pairs, making a chevron. On one end, mark from point to point. Add 1/4" for a seam allowance.

Mark   Cut

Pieced center seam

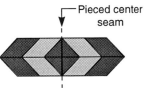

Flip half the chevron strata
and piece at the center.

Congratulations! You've finished half. Now reverse the order of the strips to make the second combination.

Finish the blocks by cutting strips and slicing squares for the center. Then sew triangles to the corners.

☑ An underlying grid

☑ Sequence of color repeats in same shape

❏ Mirror-image shapes

☑ Straight-seam sewing

❏ If none of the above help, ask yourself, Could any of these combinations of pieces fit on a strata?

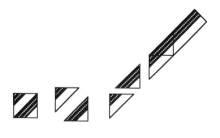

Example 4.

This sounds strange but sometimes the construction method is determined not by the block design but by the pattern on the fabric. This block pattern is shown first in two solids and then in a solid and a stripe.

Let's look at the pattern done in two solids first. At this angle, all of the lines appear to be 45° diagonals. But if you turned your head or the book 45°, the pattern lines would become 90° vertical and horizontal. Then the entire pattern could be worked with multistrip panels. Also, all sewing would be on the straight of the grain, an important feature when you have that option. You will need to analyze carefully, as there are several strip widths and panels.

Now use a stripe as in the second version of the pattern. The major construction lines must conform to the placement of the striped fabric. You cannot turn the pattern 45° and make strata that make squares. Draw lines where all of the striped fabric intersects. The pattern is now broken down into identical squares. Each square is composed of two combinations, which come from one strata.

This approach is easier to understand for some, but slower to construct, as you work with only two strips at a time. Also all the seams on the outside of the squares are on the bias, a situation I prefer to avoid.

Example 5.

These next two patterns are both similar. They're composed of vertical, horizontal, and diagonal lines. They therefore fit on a square grid. Some areas can be strip-pieced. Remaining squares and rectangles can be quick-cut. The triangles appear opposite mirror-image triangles. This is often a clue that they can be made in pairs using Crystal Piecing of Half-Square Triangles (see page 25).

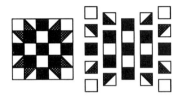 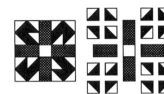

Example 6.

Some geometrical patterns don't lend themselves to the construction methods in this book. Compass-type patterns can be quick-cut, but that's about it. These patterns radiate from the center.

None of these patterns fit neatly on a grid. That's generally a giveaway that a pattern can't be quick-pieced. The parts that have mirror-image pieces could be Crystal-Pieced. Other pieces would then need to be set in. Setting in pieces is generally another giveaway clue that a pattern isn't a good candidate for quick-piecing methods.

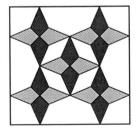 

☑ An underlying grid

☑ Sequence of color repeats in same shape

☑ Mirror-image shapes

☑ Straight-seam sewing

❏ If none of the above help, ask yourself, Could any of these combinations of pieces fit on a strata?

❏ An underlying grid

❏ Sequence of color repeats in same shape

☑ Mirror-image shapes

❏ Straight-seam sewing

❏ If none of the above help, ask yourself, Could any of these combinations of pieces fit on a strata?

I've included this pattern to illustrate that there are patterns which can be Crystal-Pieced, but aren't worth doing this way. This is another example of the saying, "Just because you can doesn't mean you should."

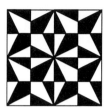

Conclusion

Good luck analyzing patterns. With practice, I know you can do it. Then all of the potential of quilt patterns will be open to you. And now, here's your pop quiz. If you can figure these out by yourself, with no instructions, you pass.

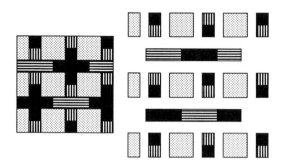

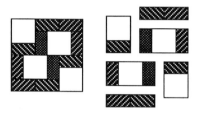

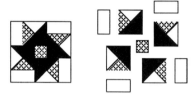

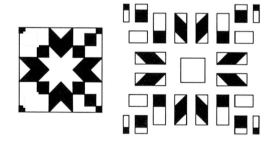

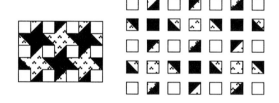

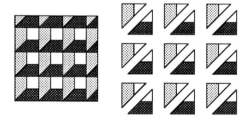

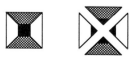

Adjust the Size

Calculating the size of a quilt is not as straightforward as looking at a chart of bed sizes, measuring the drop, and adding the pillow tuck.

For example, you may want the quilt design only on the top of the mattress, with plain fabric on the sides. You may put your pillows on top of the quilt and not need a pillow tuck. Or you may want a shortened drop.

Here are the standard mattress sizes:

Crib	30" x 75"
Twin	39" x 75"
Extra-long Twin	39" x 80"
Dual Twin	78" x 75"
Double	54" x 75"
Extra-long Double	54" x 80"
Queen	60" x 80"
King	76" x 80"
California King	72" x 84"
Your mattress:	

A good beginning in planning your design is to know how it will look on the mattress top, since that's the first thing we see. Measure the length and width of your mattress top. What size block goes evenly into the width?

For example, if you have a California-King-sized mattress and plan a quilt without a pillow tuck and a plain fabric border, you could fit the following blocks into its width and length:

Block Size	Width	Length
	72"	84"
6"	12	14
7"	10*	12
8"	9	10*
9"	8	9*
10"	7*	8*
11"	6*	7*
12"	6	7

*Part of the border will show on the top of the bed.

Figure these same measurements out for the beds in your life.

15.

Calculations: Size, Difficulty, Yardage

Once you have designed a quilt top, it's time to adjust its size for its eventual location and its difficulty in relation to the amount of time and skill you have. Then you can estimate yardage.

Give the amount of the drop you want some serious thought. Often one-half or more of the quilt is in the drop. If a full drop is not important to you, don't have one. You will save about one-third of the cost and work. Use a dust ruffle or a bedspread underneath a quilt with a short drop.

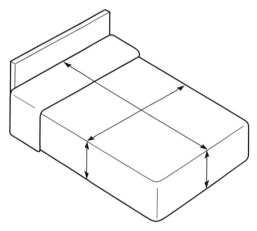

Width = Two times the drop plus the width of the mattress

Length = The drop plus the length of the mattress plus pillow tuck (optional)

Keep in mind that many quilt designs look better with an odd number of blocks in both directions. On this king-sized quilt top, for example, you might want to add one block to the width—or subtract one from the width and add the extra needed to the drop.

Or do as I do: I prefer to design a quilt, make it, and then find a place for it.

Now measure the full bed, with drop and pillow tuck. The drop is loosely defined in three sizes. (Of course you can make it whatever size you want.)

Comforter: About 14" larger than the mattress and used over the bedspread.

Coverlet: 8" to 12" larger than the mattress and used with a dust ruffle.

Bedspread: About 20" – 21" larger than the mattress. As bed frames vary in height, measure the distance from your mattress edge to a few inches short of the floor.

The pillow tuck depth depends on how many pillows it must cover and how thick they are. Again, measure your bed, using a tape measure around the pillows.

Decide on the size of your drop and tuck and add them to your mattress size.

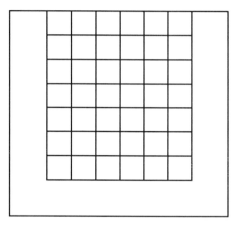

Make a sketch on graph paper of the skeleton of your quilt, showing its length and width, with placement of blocks and borders. This will help you calculate yardage later.

In planning, remember these special-purpose quilt sizes and their demands:

Baby quilts: Minimum finished size of 36" x 36".

Lap or cuddle quilts: The quilter's equivalent of an afghan, with an approximate size of 5' x 6'.

Waterbeds: Because these quilts tuck into the bed frame, plan a shorter drop and possibly no border design since it will be hidden.

Poster beds: These need square corners cut out at the bottom, so the drop will hang properly around the posts.

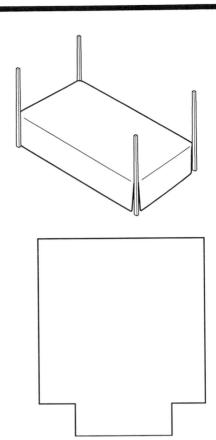

Adjust the Difficulty

While you may have gone wild designing a block in Chapter 13, reality now sets in.

In selecting a design, consider the obvious, such as what your preferences are and who it is for, but also your level of skill and how much time you have available to make the quilt.

One distinction I would like to make is between level of difficulty and amount of time. We often associate fast with easy and slow with difficult, but that is not always the case. For example, a Star of Bethlehem (see page 113) made using the strip method is fast, but diamonds are definitely not easy. The trick is to find a pattern that appears difficult, but is not, that you like, and that is relatively fast.

Level of Difficulty

Geometric shapes in Quick Quiltmaking vary as to level of difficulty. Some require more skill to mark, sew, and cut than others.

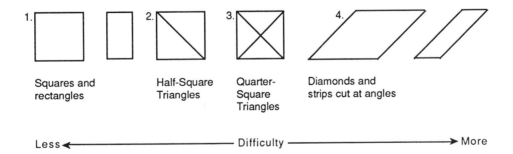

1. Squares and rectangles
2. Half-Square Triangles
3. Quarter-Square Triangles
4. Diamonds and strips cut at angles

Less ◄——————————— Difficulty ———————————► More

The size of the pieces also affects difficulty. The smaller the size, the greater the skill you need to do accurate piecing. An 1/8" error can be eased in if the pieces finish 4" or larger. The same 1/8" error cannot successfully be worked into a piece finishing 2". The amount of the error is the same but proportionally it is greater.

Amount of Time

Geometric shapes also vary in the amount of time needed to mark, sew, and cut them.

Another factor influencing the amount of time is the number of pieces in a project. The more pieces, obviously the longer it will take to piece them. I consider anything below 300 pieces a small amount and anything over 1,000 to be a lot. With experience, you may decide differently.

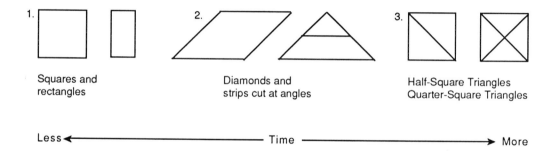

1. Squares and rectangles

2. Diamonds and strips cut at angles

3. Half-Square Triangles Quarter-Square Triangles

Less ← ———————— Time ————————→ More

Changing a Quilt's Size

What if you see a quilt pattern you like, but the directions are not for the size quilt you need? Here are some ways of changing the quilt to the size you want and their effect on difficulty and time.

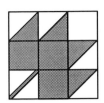
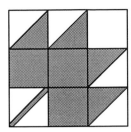

Increase or Decrease the Scale of the Pattern

Use the same number of pieces, but make each piece larger or smaller. (Don't increase the scale too much or it will look out of proportion with the rest of the furnishings in the room.)

Effect on Difficulty

Increasing the scale makes for easier piecing.

Decreasing the scale makes for more difficult piecing.

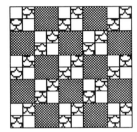

Effect on Time

Decrease the scale and the quilt top will take longer to make because you will have more pieces.

Increase the scale and the quilt top will be made more quickly due to having less pieces.

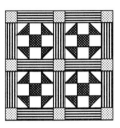

Add or Subtract Blocks or Rows

If you want to keep the scale of the pattern the same, you can make more or less blocks or rows, but the nature of the setting determines how many.

If the design alternates pieced with plain blocks, add or subtract rows two at a time.

If the design includes lattice strips, add or subtract a row of blocks and a row of lattice strips.

If the design is set continuously, add or subtract a row of blocks.

Effect on Difficulty

None

Effect on Time

Increased or decreased in proportion to amount added or decreased.

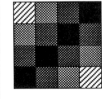

People often ask me how much material it takes to make a quilt without even having a specific quilt in mind! That is like asking how much a house costs, how tall a tree is, or any other general question. Before being able to determine the yardage for any quilt, three questions must be answered

1. What size is the mattress?

2. How big is the drop (and pillow tuck if desired)?

3. What is the scale of the design?

Shoo Fly

Add Borders

Make the quilt as directed, but add a border or borders. These can range from fabric strips to intricate pieced borders. A simple fabric strip or several of them is the easiest way to make a quilt larger.

Effect on Difficulty
Varies with the complexity of the border.

Effect on Time
Also varies with the complexity of the border.

Determine Yardage

Now that you have a quilt design and a graph paper plan, here are three methods to calculate yardage. The method you use depends on whether you are going out to buy new material for a specific quilt or if you are buying ahead for a presently undetermined quilt. This often happens when you have nothing specific in mind, but find a good buy on a particular fabric that you just must have. These days, too, people buy ahead to fill in their color palette, then design a quilt.

If you do not want to do the math, ask the quilt shop where you bought your fabric to help you figure your yardage. It is one of the services they provide.

Method 1: Buy a lot of fabric

A favored method of myself and others is to buy too much in the first place. Purchase at least three yards if there will be several colors used, five yards if two colors will be used.

Method 2: Calculate precisely

In this method, you figure yardage for each shape and each fabric, then add everything up.

1. Determine how many of a particular shape of one fabric are in a whole quilt. Let's start with the white square in this 12" Shoo Fly Block. This quilt has 35 blocks. Each block has four white squares that finish 4".

$$4 \times 35 = 140$$

2. Add the seam allowance to the shape.

$$4" + 1/4" + 1/4" = 4\text{-}1/2" \text{ square}$$

3. Count or determine mathematically how many will fit into a yard, both across and lengthwise. I'm being conservative here about width. You may be able to squeeze more inches out of a 44"-wide fabric. I'd rather be safe than sorry. Always round down. (Using a calculator makes it easier, but you have to convert decimals to fractions and vice versa.)

36" length ÷ 4-1/2" = 8 squares possible per yard

40" width ÷ 4-1/2" = 8 squares possible across the material

8 x 8 = 64, the number of white squares you can cut from one yard

4. Divide the number from Step 3 into the total white squares in the whole quilt (from Step 1).

140 ÷ 64 = 2.1875 or 2-1/4 yards

For good measure, round up 1/8 yard to 2-3/8 yards.

5. Repeat with each shape and with each color. The charts of Half- and Quarter-Square Triangles yields on pages 233 – 234 should help with some shapes. Keep a chart of colors like that shown at right.

6. Add up the yardage requirement for each color.

The formula for what you've just done is

Yardage =

cut size x the total number of this piece in this color in whole quilt divided by

---

the number of pieces that fit the width and length of a yard

Congratulations if you made it through with full comprehension. This or some variation of it is the traditional way of figuring yardage. This method is very accurate, slow, tedious, and uses a great deal of basic math. There is no guessing with this method. You will know exactly how much you will need. Do allow a little extra.

Method 3: Calculate a percentage

In this method you calculate the square footage of your quilt as if it were a whole piece of fabric thrown over the bed. Then you adjust up by a percent to account for seam allowances in the pieced quilt. We'll use the same 12" Shoo Fly Block.

1. Determine the finished size of one shape: 4".

2. Add in the seam allowance.

4" +1/4" + 1/4" = 4-1/2" square

3. Calculate the square inches per square, both finished and cut, by multiplying the finished size by itself and the cut size by itself.

4" x 4" = 16

4-1/2" x 4-1/2" = 20-1/4"

4. On a percentage basis, how much larger is the piece with the seam allowance than the finished piece? To calculate, divide the answers to Step 3 into each other. You are always dividing the smaller number into the larger number. Move the decimal

Quilt Questions

Ask yourself:

What sizes of blocks or pieces are most easily worked? 6", 8", 9", 10", 12", 15"

How many blocks will fit in my width? Length?

Does the quilt design determine the ratio of length to width?

Is this a square quilt?

Can I add or subtract blocks/rows?

Do I want a lattice? How wide?

Do I want a border?

How difficult is the piecing?

How much time do I have?

Are my sewing skills up to this much work?

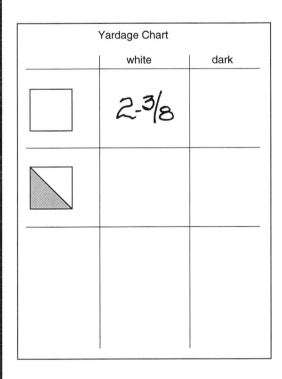

Chapter 15. **Calculations** | **231**

point two steps to the right to get the percentage and round off. (But keep track of the first answer. You'll need it in Step 6.)

20-1/4" ÷ 16 = 1.27 = 127%

5. How many square inches are in your quilt top? Multiply width times length and divide by 1440 (this assumes a useable fabric width of 40" x 36" long = 1440 square inches). The answer is the number of yards you need before piecing.

60" (five 12" blocks) x 84" (seven 12" blocks) = 5040 ÷ 1440 = 3.5 or 3-1/2 yards

6. Increase the number of yards in the surface area of your quilt by the percentage determined in Step 4. This is easier to do in decimals. (Move the decimal point back to the left two steps to convert the percent from Step 4 to decimal.) The answer should always be bigger than the number with which you started.

3.5 x 1.27 = 4.5 or 4-1/2 yards

7. Examine your design. In what proportion are the colors used? If you have a repeating design, you only need examine one block. The same proportions hold for the entire quilt, unless you are adding borders or lattices, which demand more fabric in those colors. In the Shoo Fly Block, there are nine squares. Four of them are Half-Square Triangles. If you count the four dark triangles with themselves instead of with white triangles and vice versa for the white triangles, you come up with three dark squares and six white squares for a total of nine squares.

The proportion of white to dark is 2/3 to 1/3.

8. Multiply the answer in Step 6 by one of the proportions you determined in Step 7. This is easier to do in decimals.

4.5 x .66 = 2.97 or 3 yards white

4.5 x .33 = 1.49 or 1-1/2 yards dark

Double-check your answer. Do they add up close to the figure from Step 6?

This is a relatively fast method, especially if you round off all numbers, but it's somewhat less accurate than Method 2. It is most appropriate when there are only one or two shapes. Be sure to buy generously, to allow for shrinkage, unuseable areas, etc.

If you are always making the same-sized quilts for the same beds, you only need to calculate the square inches once for each quilt and its bed. Keep the figures on file. Then you'll always have a starting point for how much yardage that bed needs just to cover it plain.

Decimal Conversion for Yard

inches	yard	decimal
4-1/2	1/8	.125
9	1/4	.25
12	1/3	.33
13-1/2	3/8	.375
18	1/2	.5
22-1/2	5/8	.625
24	2/3	.66
27	3/4	.75

Barbara Johannah's Crystal Piecing

Yields

These charts show the likely maximum number of pieces possible (not including selvage) from 45"-wide fabric. Allow extra for shrinking, uneven cut ends, etc.

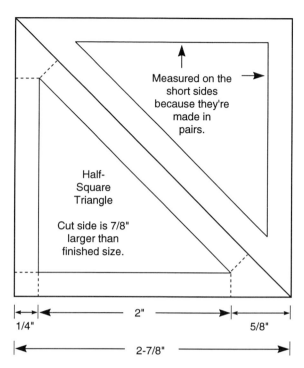

Half-Square Triangle

Cut side is 7/8" larger than finished size.

Measured on the short sides because they're made in pairs.

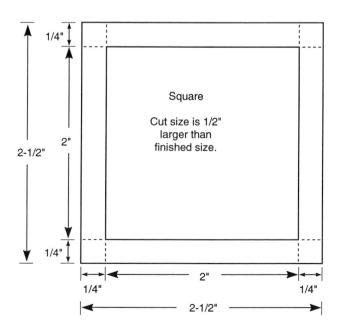

Square

Cut size is 1/2" larger than finished size.

Half-Square Triangles

Number of Squares	Finished Size	Seam Allowance (inches)	Marked Size	Length in Yards- 45" width	Number of Pieces
378	1	1/4	1-7/8	1	756
340	1-1/8	1/4	2	1	680
154	2	1/4	2-7/8	1	308
143	2-1/8	1/4	3	1	286
80	3	1/4	3-7/8	1	160
80	3-1/8	1/4	4	1	160
48	4	1/4	4-7/8	1	96
48	4-1/8	1/4	5	1	96
35	5	1/4	5-7/8	1	70
35	5-1/8	1/4	6	1	70
30	6	1/4	6-7/8	1	60
30	6-1/8	1/4	7	1	60
20	7	1/4	7-7/8	1	40
20	7-1/8	1/4	8	1	40
12	8	1/4	8-7/8	7/8	24
12	8-1/8	1/4	9	7/8	24
12	9	1/4	9-7/8	7/8	24
12	9-1/8	1/4	10	7/8	24
12	10	1/4	10-7/8	1	24
12	10-1/8	1/4	11	1	24

Equilateral Triangles
(Stagger strips 2-1/2")

Finished Size	Seam Allowance (inches)	Strip width	Length in Yards- 45" width	Number of Pieces
2"	1/4"	2-1/2"	1"	91

Squares

Finished Size	Seam Allowance (inches)	Marked Size (inches)	Length in Yards- 45" width	Number of Pieces
1"	1/4"	1-1/2"	1	572
2"	1/4"	2-1/2"	1	208
3"	1/4"	3-1/2"	1	108
4"	1/4"	4-1/2"	1	63
5"	1/4"	5-1/2"	1	42
6"	1/4"	6-1/2"	1	30
7"	1/4"	7-1/2"	1	20
8"	1/4"	8-1/2"	1	20
9"	1/4"	9-1/2"	7/8	12
10"	1/4"	10-1/2"	1	12
11"	1/4"	11-1/2"	3/4	6
12"	1/4"	12-1/2"	3/4	6

Yields

Quarter-Square Triangles

Finished Size	Seam Allowance (inches)	Marked Size	Length in Yards-45" width	Number of Pieces	Number of Squares
3/4	1/4	2	1	1280	320
1	1/4	2-1/4	1	1008	252
1-3/4	1/4	3	1	616	154
2	1/4	3-1/4	1	520	130
2-3/4	1/4	4	1	320	80
3	1/4	4-1/4	1	320	80
3-3/4	1/4	5	1	192	48
4	1/4	5-1/4	1	192	48
4-3/4	1/4	6	1	120	30
5	1/4	6-1/4	1	120	30
5-3/4	1/4	7	7/8	96	24
6	1/4	7-1/4	7/8	96	24
6-3/4	1/4	8	1	80	20
7	1/4	8-1/4	1	80	20
7-3/4	1/4	9	7/8	48	12
8	1/4	9-1/4	7/8	48	12
8-3/4	1/4	10	7/8	48	12
9	1/4	10-1/4	1	48	12
9-3/4	1/4	11	1	36	9
10	1/4	11-1/4	1	36	9

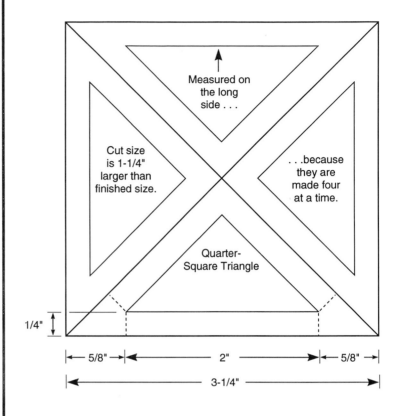

Measured on the long side . . .

Cut size is 1-1/4" larger than finished size.

. . .because they are made four at a time.

Quarter-Square Triangle

1/4"

5/8" 2" 5/8"

3-1/4"

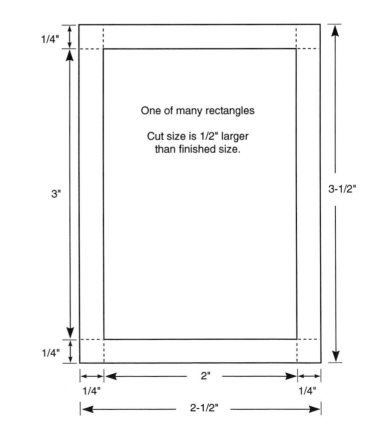

One of many rectangles

Cut size is 1/2" larger than finished size.

1/4"

3"

3-1/2"

1/4"

1/4" 2" 1/4"

2-1/2"

Part Six:
Barbara's Notebook

The following pages are facsimiles from my notebooks. Years ago I started making them because I would forget what I had come up with previously. I wanted a way of visiting my previous thoughts. I have 1/4" graph-paper notebooks and 60°-triangle notebooks and cut-and-paste notebooks.

I don't critique my ideas before putting them down on paper. I don't second-guess myself. I just let the thoughts come.

I usually start with patterns and ask myself how I could construct them with Crystal Piecing or Strips and Strata. My drawings are often cryptic, even to me. Lots end up in the garbage can.

But I'm including some of them here to spark thinking in others. I hope these ideas will be vehicles for exploring new methods.

Warning: Not everything in this section works; not everything is proportional. From brilliant to half-baked to totally off-base, these are my thoughts as they first came to me.

Practice Seeing Shapes Fit Efficiently on a Grid

Barbara Johannah's Crystal Piecing

Rotation

of Two Strip

Equilateral Triangle Combinations

* also a reflection

Use a Mirror to Turn Corners

At first a mirror is helpful in turning corners. With _____ mirror practice you can do without it.

mirror

Easy
Interlocking Rings
no mitering

mirror
45°

To make a 60° pattern fit a 90° corner, hold the mirror at a 45° angle. Cut and paste to fit.

Two Strip
60°

Interlocking Rings
mitter intersections

These two fit inside
Interlocking Rings

240   Barbara Johannah's Crystal Piecing

Same as ⬚ (HST) & ⊠ (QST)
mark, sew, cut

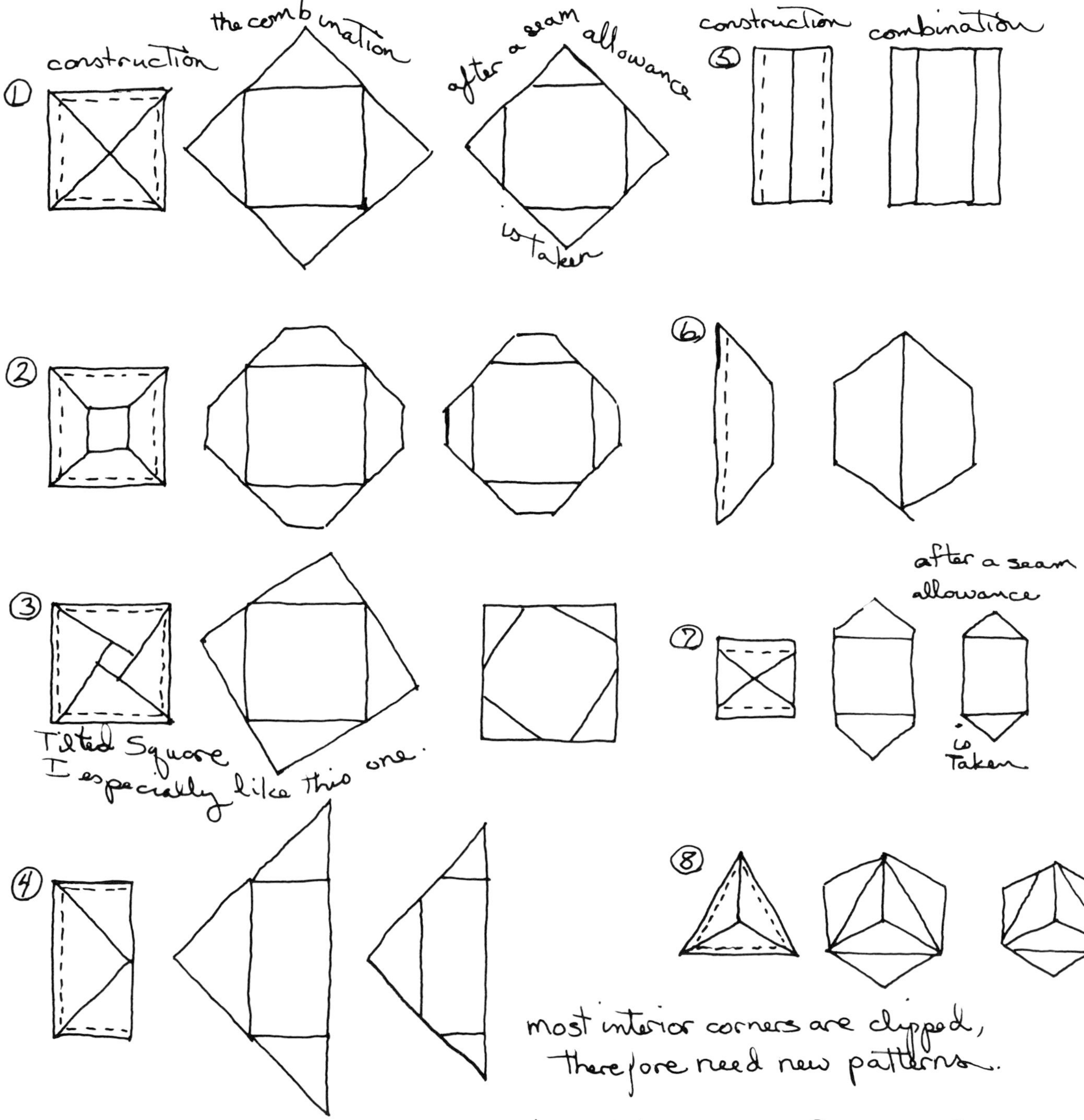

Crystal Piecing Possibilities

① construction — the combination — after a seam allowance is taken

⑤ construction — the combination

②

⑥

③ Tilted Square
I especially like this one.

⑦ after a seam allowance — is Taken

④

⑧ most interior corners are clipped, therefore need new patterns.

some cut lines need to be adjusted because of unequal angles to create finished straight lines.
Some can be set as is, some need fill in pieces to be sewn together with straight line sewing.

Plain Top Crystal Piecing
New Shapes - New Combinations - New Blocks

To get this: Do this:

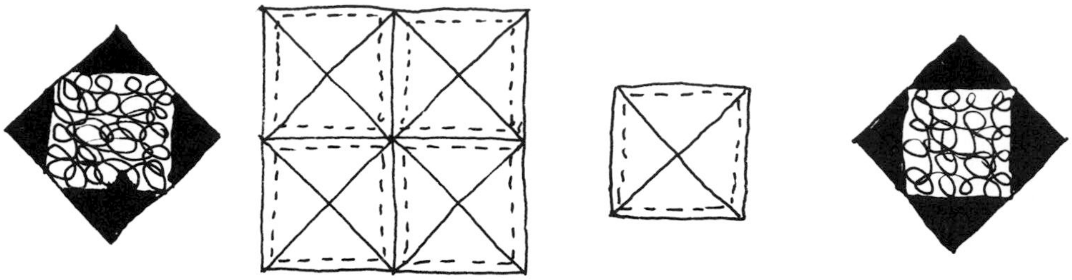

after seam allowance is taken

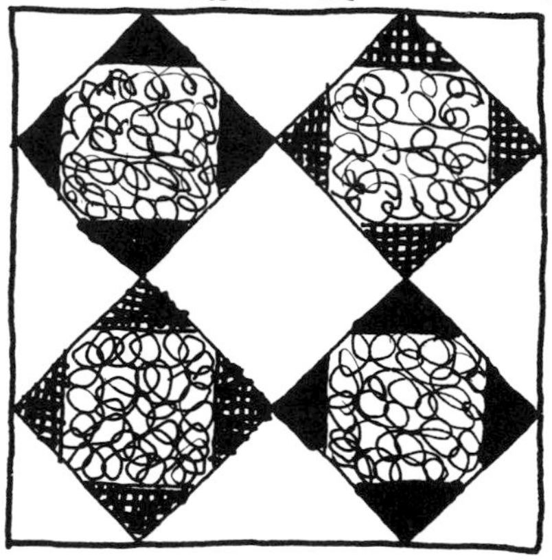

all sides will be bias and I like to avoid working with bias cut fabric if I can.

★ Colette Wolff suggested placing the top fabric on the bias. After it is sewn and cut it will then be straight grain!

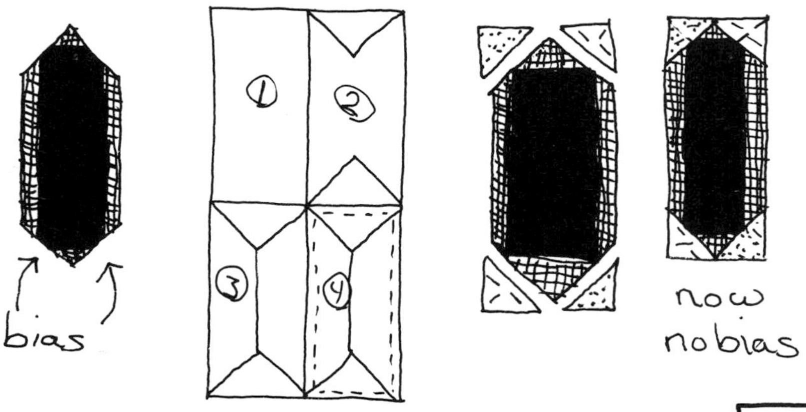

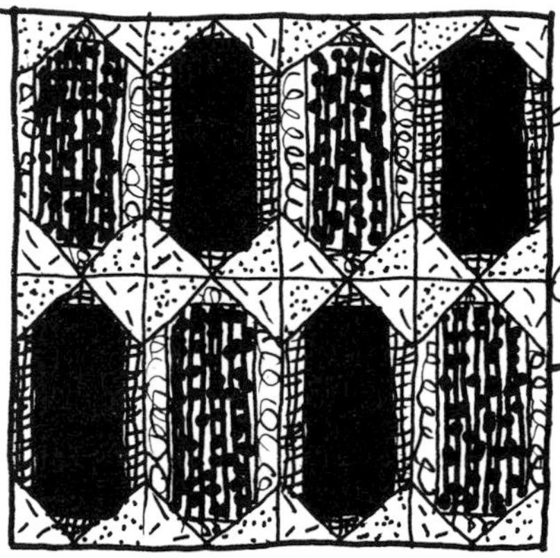

bias

now no bias

or

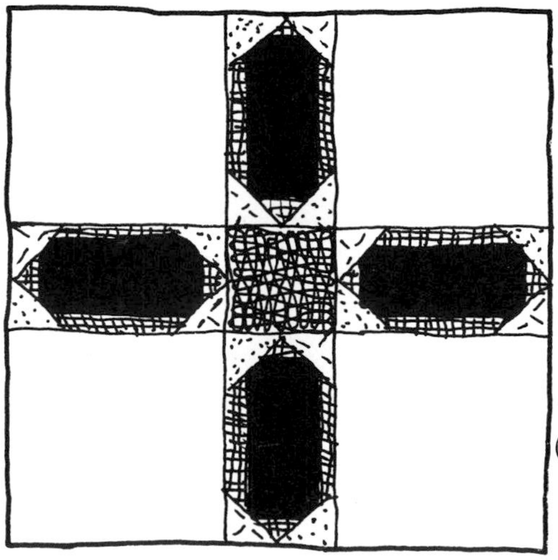

Squaring up the blocks for easier sewing.

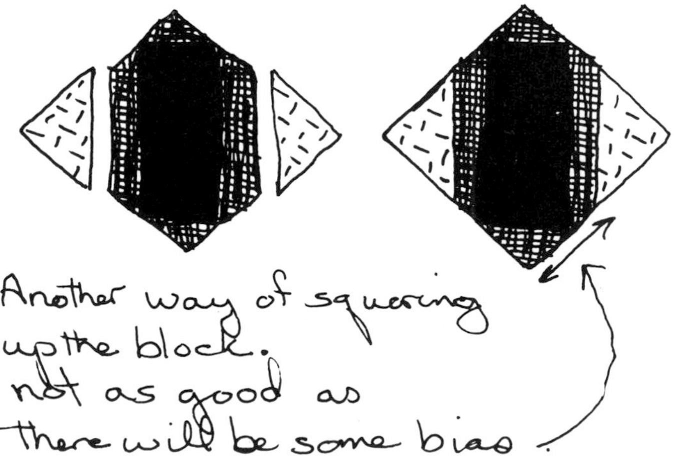

Another way of squaring up the block. not as good as there will be some bias.

Pieced Top Crystal Piecing
New Shapes - New Combinations - New Blocks

To get this: Do this:

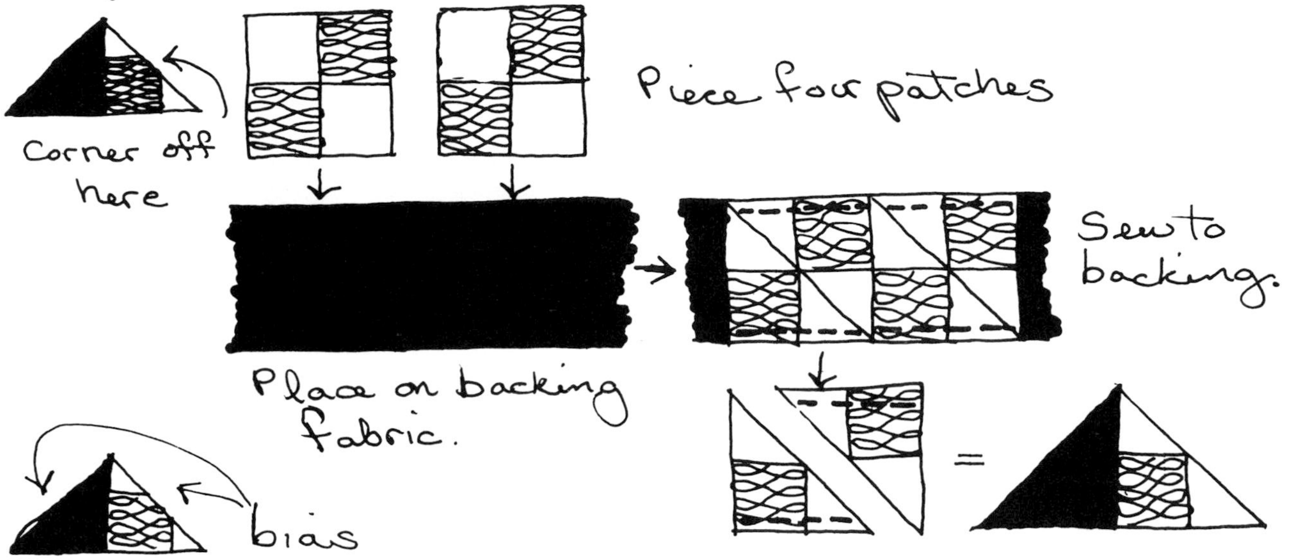

Corner off here

Piece four patches

Place on backing fabric.

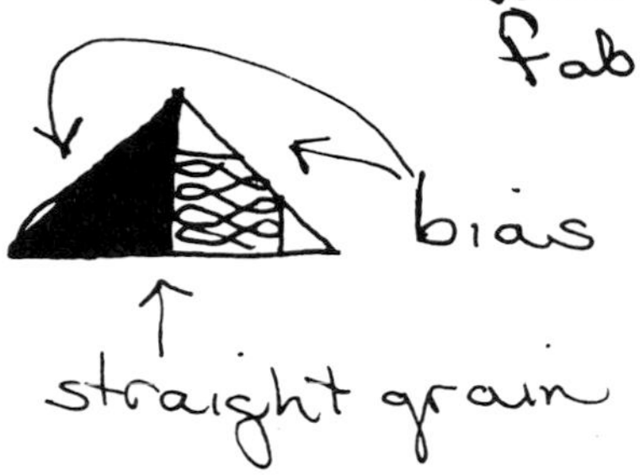

Sew to backing.

bias

↑ straight grain

+

=

||

Double four patch extension of above

Sew diagonally
no bias

no bias

no bias

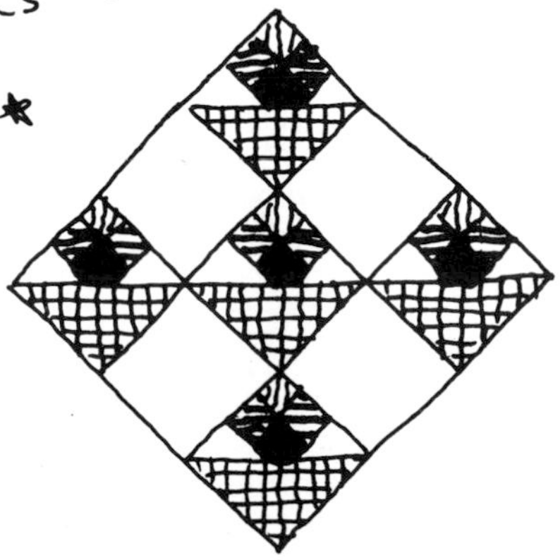

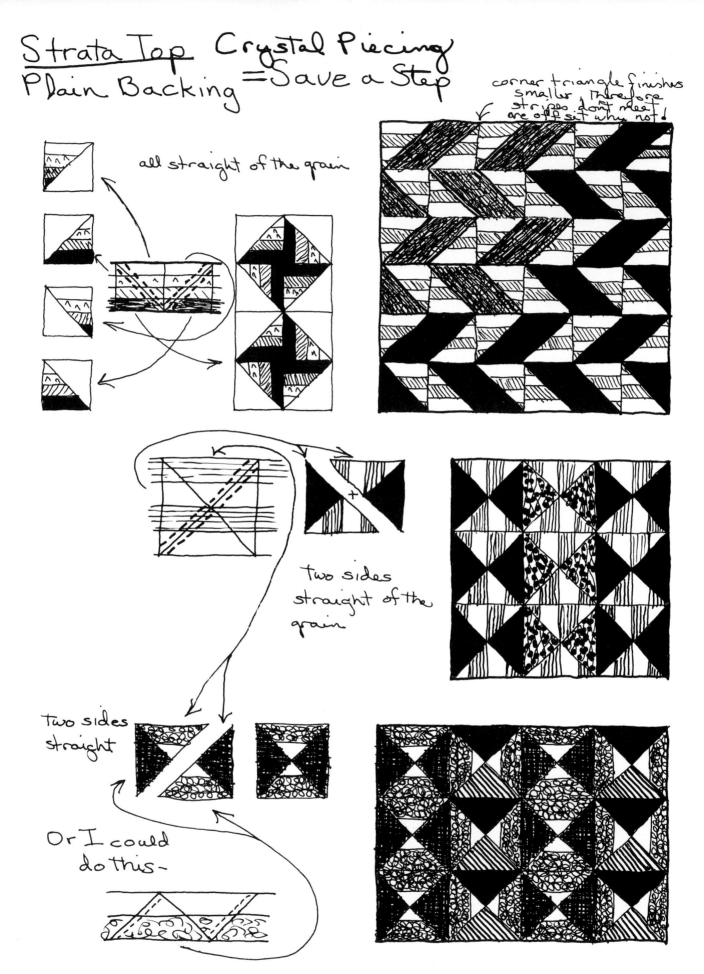

Strata Top Crystal Piecing
Plain Backing = Save a Step

corner triangle finishes smaller, therefore stripes don't meet are offset why not!

all straight of the grain

two sides straight of the grain

two sides straight

Or I could do this—

45° Grid

Grids **245**

60° Grid

Index

Other Books by Barbara Johannah

Quick Quilting / Make a Quilt This Weekend
(out of print)

Quick Quiltmaking Handbook
$8.95, soft cover, 8-1/2 x 11, 128 pages, profusely illustrated

Continuous Curve Quilting
Machine Quilting the Pieced Quilt Top
$8.95, soft cover, 8-1/2 x 11, 56 pages, profusely illustrated

Half Square Triangles
Exploring Design
$14.95, soft cover, 8-1/2 x 11, 80 pages, 16 pages of color and black and white how-to photos, hundreds of drawings

The above books are available from:

Purchase for Less
231 Floresta BJB
Portola Valley, CA 94028

Are you interested in a quarterly newsletter about creative uses of the sewing machine and serger? Write to *The Creative Machine*-BJ, PO Box 2634, Menlo Park, CA 94026.